Contents

Introduction 1

Part I: The Universe 101 7
   1. The Physical Universe 8
   2. The Metaphysical Universe 14

Part II: Harnessing Your Inner Power 24
   3. Elements of Inner Power 25
   4. Universal Law 28
   5. Intention 37
   6. Intuition 41
   7. Imagination 48
   8. The Philosopher's Stone 53

Part III: The Science of Manifesting 62
   9. The Five-Step Manifesting Method 63
      Step 1. Intention 66
      Step 2. Impression 71
      Step 3. Surrender 83
      Step 4. Illumination 88
      Step 5. Inspired Action 94

Part IV: Manifesting Your Higher Purpose 102
   10. Awakening to Higher Purpose 103
   11. Discovering Your Higher Purpose 111
   12. Realizing Your Higher Purpose 121

The Alchemist's Toolkit 133

Introduction

Some have declared that it lies within our choice to gaze continually upon a world of equal or even greater wonder and beauty. It is said by these that the experiments of the alchemists are, in fact, related not to the transmutation of metals, but to the transmutation of the entire universe. This method, or art, or science, or whatever we choose to call it, is simply concerned to restore the delights of the primal paradise; to enable men, if they will, to inhabit a world of joy and splendor. It is perhaps possible that there is such an experiment, and that there are some who have made it.

- Richard Rolle de Hampole, 1380

The Purpose of this Book

My intention in writing this book is to help you to become an alchemist in your own life – to help you find your life's gold. In it, you will learn powerful principles and methods that will enable you to *create* tremendous abundance and financial prosperity.

If you have ever tried to operate the Law of Attraction, you, like many, have probably met with unsatisfactory results. It is a fickle and passive principle; it is not the cause of prosperity. Rather than waiting around for a financial windfall or other miraculous good fortune, you can set about actively creating it by aligning with your Higher Purpose.

Therefore, before you begin this book, I ask that you put aside everything you know about the Law of Attraction, affirmations and positive thinking. They are a long and winding road to creating abundance, because they do not leverage the real cause of prosperity.

In this book, you will learn that the secret to creating abundance is not a secret at all – it is startlingly obvious. The key is to serve others with your special talents and passions; that is, to align with your Higher Purpose. In this way, you will create a prosperity consciousness by adding tremendous value to others' lives, which allows them to reward you in kind.

If you want to create money and prosperity, you must find or create value. After all, money is just a store of value. The most powerful and effective way to create value is by serving others through your Higher Purpose. By virtue of immutable laws of exchange, you must receive back the value you create for others.

This book will equip you on your journey to becoming an alchemist by helping you to:

- ✧ Understand the metaphysical principles that govern the Universe
- ✧ Learn how to harness your Inner Power through intention, intuition and imagination
- ✧ Discover how to tap into Universal intelligence, and allow creative inspiration to flow to you
- ✧ Master a powerful five-step manifesting method
- ✧ Align with your Higher Purpose by discovering your special talents and passions.

Your journey toward the realization of your Higher Purpose is an enriching and rewarding one. You will infuse yourself with purpose, passion and a sense of mission along the way. Whether you are well progressed along this path, or your journey has just begun, there is much to learn and yet more to do.

How to Use this Book

If this book is your first encounter with metaphysical concepts and principles, I encourage you to break through the initial resistance that their unfamiliarity may cause. Initially, as with any new subject you learn, you should first read it casually without getting deeply involved. After you have absorbed the foundations, you can re-read it and allow the concepts to crystallize further.

The metaphysical foundations are critical, because they serve as a framework for understanding. Many books simply offer a method with little explanation as to how and why they work. However, you will have much more success with a method when you have a comprehensive understanding of how it works.

Just like driving a car, you need to understand the controls. You learn how to start it, engage the clutch, accelerate and brake. So too, each element of your Inner Power controls a different aspect of the manifesting process. Moreover, when you stall the manifesting process, you need to know how to start it back up again!

I strongly recommend that you read Parts I, II & III in sequence. This is because each part builds upon concepts and principles of the preceding part. Part IV, on the other hand, is largely self-contained and can be read at your leisure.

Book Outline

Part I: The Universe 101

The Universe 101 shows you how the early Universe was formed, how the matter in the physical Universe is created, and what fundamental principles the non-physical, or metaphysical, Universe are governed by. You will also learn about the most powerful law in the metaphysical Universe – The Law of Focus.

Part II: Elements of Inner Power

In this part, you will learn about the elements of your Inner Power – intention, intuition and imagination – and discover how to become receptive to intuitive guidance and command the unbounded power of your imagination. You will also learn how to forge the Philosopher's Stone, which is a catalyst for exponentially increasing your Inner Power.

Part III: The Science of Manifesting

In The Science of Manifesting, you will learn a highly effective five-step method aimed at leveraging and mastering your Inner Power. You will also learn about manifesting concepts such as synchronicity, expectancy and faith.

Part IV: Your Higher Purpose

In this part, you will learn how about the process of awakening to your Higher Purpose. Through introspective questions about your passions and talents, you will begin to get clarity about your Higher Purpose. You will formulate a Divine Mission Statement, and learn practical tips on realizing it with the five-step manifesting method detailed in Part III.

Part I

The Universe 101

The Physical Universe –
The Metaphysical Universe

Chapter One

The Physical Universe

*In some sense man is a microcosm of the universe;
therefore what man is, is a clue to the universe.
We are enfolded in the universe.*
- David Bohm

In this chapter, you will learn about the creation of the physical Universe. The Universe is the ultimate alchemist and has much to teach us in our quest for gold. It will also give you a glimpse of the vast intelligence that orchestrates the symphony of life. Only when you understand what happened to get us from nowhere to now here can you appreciate the vast magnificence of the Universe's intelligence. Let us start by looking at where it all began, and how matter and mind fit into the bigger picture.

In The Beginning

Around 13.7 billion years ago, the most unimaginably profound thing happened. The Universe crossed the threshold from formlessness into form. Energy and matter, gravity, space and time all coalesced in an explosion of incomprehensible magnitude. The physical Universe was born. A hundred thousand years worth of inquiry and contemplation later, and we still have no explanation for why it happened or what caused it. Nevertheless, we do have a solid understanding of the events that must have taken place since the Big Bang to give us the world we see today.

The Early Universe

In the moments following the Big Bang, the Universe expanded into a super heated primordial soup of subatomic particles. After the early Universe cooled down, it was comprised mainly of hydrogen and helium, the two simplest elements in the Universe.

Over billions of years, and under the influence of gravity, these vast gas clouds began to condense together. Eventually, these 'clumps' of gas became so dense and hot that they would collapse under their own weight. This results in the release of tremendous amounts of energy and a chain of events that starts the nuclear fusion process, called 'stellar ignition'.

Up to this point, we have hydrogen, helium and gravity interacting to create a fusion reaction resulting in the birth of stars. But we know the Universe is much more than burning stars undergoing fusion reactions. So what is the role of stars in the creation of the physical Universe?

Stars Create Matter

Did you know that massive stars are nature's matter manufacturing plants? There is an incredible abundance of these matter production lines throughout the Universe. In fact, latest supercomputer estimates indicate that there are seventy thousand million million million, or, seventy sextillion stars. To give you an idea of the vastness of that number, there are ten times as many stars as there are grains of sand on all the world's beaches and deserts. If running grains of sand through your hands at the beach fails to give you an appreciation of this vastness, consider that our own galaxy, the Milky Way, is but one of five hundred billion galaxies.

So, how do we go from stars to matter? This fascinating process, which scientists refer to as nucleosynthesis, is the result of the nuclear reactions fuelling the stars. We can call it Cosmic Alchemy as nature literally transmutes one element into another through nuclear fusion.

We already know that hydrogen and helium have fused together and started the process. Over time, the nuclear reactions cause the formation of progressively heavier elements, including neon, silicon and iron. In fact, a star can produce elements that have up to 26 protons, which is equivalent to iron. The following diagram shows the onion-like layering of elements that form within a star over millions of years:

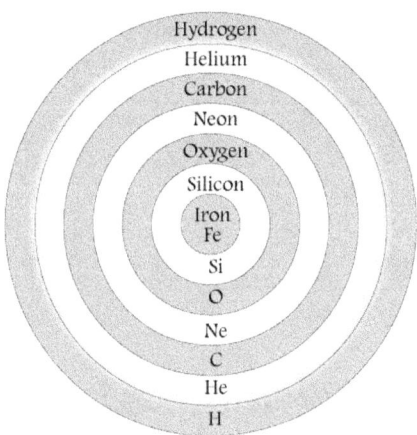

Layering of elements within a star

This, however, is not the whole story. As you can see by this periodic table, there is a whole spectrum of elements beyond Iron (Fe).

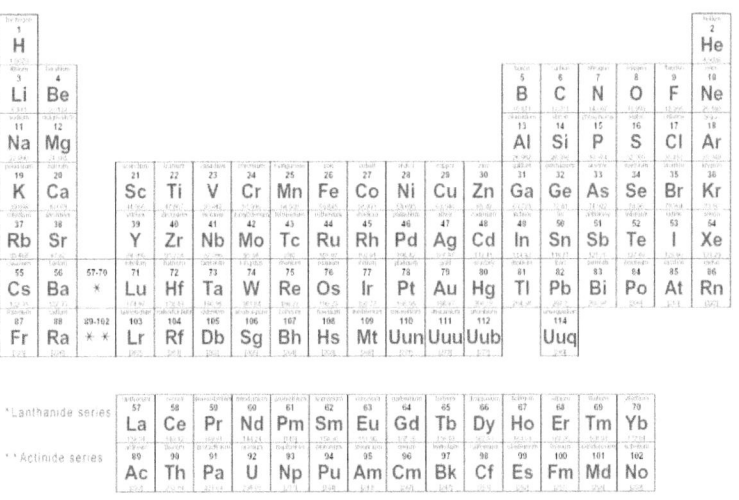

The Periodic Table of the Elements

So, what about all of the elements that are comprised of more than 26 protons? What about the alchemists' fabled elements, lead and gold? Look again at the periodic table above you will see that gold has 79 protons. How do we account for its presence?

Well, nature is the ultimate Alchemist. It does not run up against production brick walls; it goes straight through them in a most spectacular way.

Creation through Destruction

Massive stars, those around twenty times larger than our sun, eventually run out of fuel after burning for billions of years. When this happens, the star can no longer generate the heat required for the nuclear reactions. Consequently, the mass of the star collapses in upon itself, with billions of years of existence obliterated in mere seconds. The ensuing explosion, called a supernova, generates more energy than our sun would in over ten billion years.

Before shedding a tear for the star, know that in nature, destruction precedes creation. Because of the tremendous energy released by the explosion, something very special happens. In a process called supernova nucleosynthesis, the atoms fuse to one another effortlessly, transmuting lighter elements into dozens of heavier elements and Eureka! We have our gold!

Vast clouds and elemental remnants of the explosion are scattered throughout space at tremendous velocity. Over time, gravity will act upon these elements and causing them to clump together. Eventually, they will form planets such as those in our own solar system. These elements are the building blocks of the physical Universe and the foundations for life.

So let us recap the story so far. We have gone from primordial soup, to gases and gravity, to stars, to supernovas and stardust, and finally to planets. Therefore, we have planets, like Earth, that have all the precursors required to support life. So how does life evolve from here?

To complete our picture of the Universe, we must consider the other half of the equation. That is, the Universe beyond matter and physical forces such as gravity. This is the domain of the metaphysical Universe, which is simply the reality beyond what is perceptible to our physical senses.

Chapter Two

The Metaphysical Universe

*If the doors of perception were cleansed,
everything would appear to man as it is, infinite.*
- William Blake

Metaphysics is the study of laws that govern the non-physical Universe, such as Spirit, mind and intelligence. The physical Universe is actually a reflection, or projection, of the metaphysical Universe. The metaphysical Universe was around long before the Big Bang gave rise to the physical Universe. Indeed, it is the cause of the physical Universe; mind creates matter, not the other way round.

To get to the heart of metaphysics, contemplate for a moment these questions:

1. Whose idea was it to have these primordial gas clouds clump together, ignite and then explode?

2. Who devised the ingenious method to create almost a hundred known natural elements from just hydrogen, helium and gravity?
3. What is orchestrating all of that stardust into such sophisticated and complex forms of life?

The answers to these questions do not reside in the physical Universe; they are answerable only within the context of the metaphysical Universe - of Spirit, mind and intelligence. All three of these things are just different aspects of the same vast, expansive, unbounded and infinitely creative intelligence.

The flawless coordination of nucleosynthesis reactions and exploding stars are just one expression of that intelligence. Indeed, the mechanics by which the nuclear processes occur have only come within the scope of human comprehension in the past fifty years.

If you only looked at the physical Universe, the conclusion about life and its purpose would be straightforward: none of us should be here and this is all a cosmic accident and life has no meaning. This is a common view held by people who spend their entire lives studying the physical Universe, and it is a reasonable conclusion based upon the objective world with which they are concerned.

Nevertheless, to go from stardust to highly intelligent human beings is an incomprehensible leap. Make no mistake, in spite of appearances, there is an infinite intelligence orchestrating these primal building blocks into profoundly sophisticated structures. This intelligence expresses itself into form to give us the world we experience, and the minds and bodies with which to experience it.

Now, it is time to consider a remarkable concept that allows us to put the metaphysical realm into a simple framework.

Holons

The term holon was coined in 1967 by Hungarian philosopher Arthur Koestler in his book "The Ghost in the Machine". The word holon is derived from the Greek word *holos*, which means 'whole'. It also adds the suffix 'on', as in proton or neutron, which suggests a particle or part. So what is a holon?

As the name suggests, a holon is a whole/part. It is something that is a whole unto itself whilst, simultaneously, being a contributing part of another 'whole'.

The essential feature of holons is that they are systems nested within one another. To clarify the concept, take this book as an example. The letters are parts of words, but they are also self-complete as letters. Letters are parts of words, and words are parts of sentences. That is, letters are 'wholes' within themselves and 'parts' of the next higher level of wholeness, words. The same is true of words in relation to sentences and so on to paragraphs, chapters and beyond. This concept applies to everything, not just text.

Every system is a holon; from subatomic particles to atoms to molecules to galaxies and even the entire Universe as a whole. Quarks and leptons are parts of atoms, atoms are parts of molecules, and molecules are parts of the Universe. That is, they are all self-complete wholes, whilst also being a part of a more encompassing whole.

We call this organization of holons, or whole/parts, a holarchy. A holarchy is simply a hierarchy of holons. The following diagram represents the holarchy of a book:

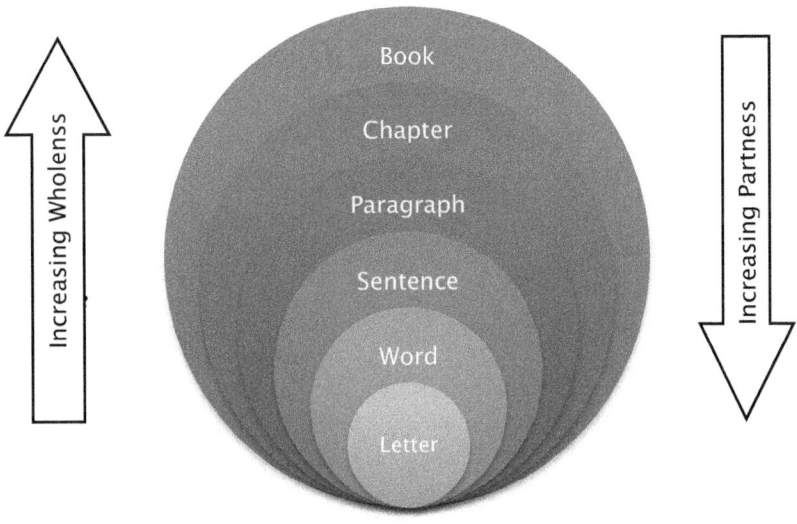

The Holarchy of a Book

Note that as you move your point of focus up or down the holarchy, your perception of what is a whole and what is a part will also change.

Everything in the Universe is a holon and is organized into a holarchy. It is the sub-structure of the entire Universe, both metaphysical and physical.

OPPOSING DRIVES OF HOLONS

Before we look at how the metaphysical Universe fits into the framework of holons, you should understand an important implication of the whole/part structure of the Universe. That is, because a holon is a whole *and* a part, it has two opposing drives. It has a drive to preserve its *partness*, and a drive to integrate into *wholeness*. The following diagram illustrates these opposing forces:

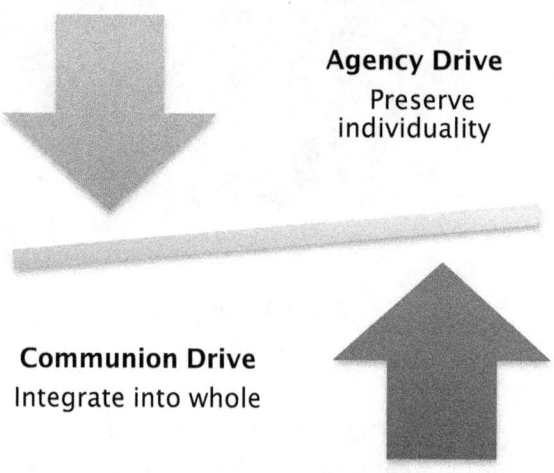

Opposing Drives of Holons

These drives give rise to the eternal battle between the Ego and Spirit, our partness and our wholeness. Put simply, the aspect of our Self that seeks to:

- **Preserve** our **individuality** is our **Egoic** or lower self.
- **Integrate** into **wholeness** is our **Spiritual** or Higher Self.

The following table gives a clearer picture of the result of these competing drives.

Individuality	Wholeness
Agency Drive	Communion Drive
Ego	Spirit
Lower Self	Higher Self
Serve yourself	Serve others
Self-Preservation	Integration

THE HOLARCHY OF MIND

Holons are systems nested within each other. This is true for every system and there are no exceptions. We can even think of the metaphysical Universe, of Spirit and mind, within the framework of holons. Mind is comprised of interacting parts that form an integrated whole, therefore mind is a holon. Mind consists of thought, perception, memory, emotion, will and imagination. Mind flows through consciousness, or awareness. The following diagram represents the structure of the metaphysical Universe:

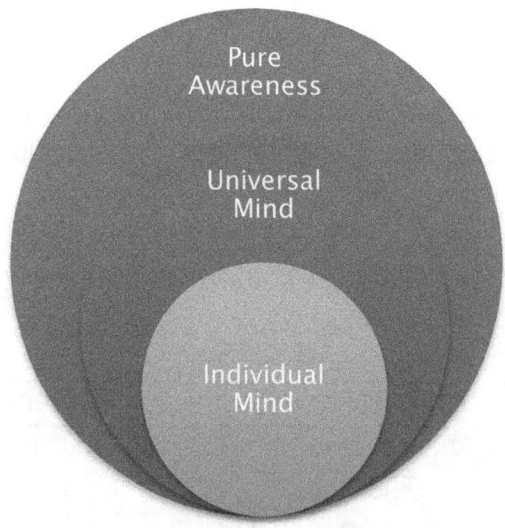

The Holarchy of Mind

There are two levels of mind, encapsulated by Pure Awareness itself. Universal Mind includes and transcends the individual mind. That is, individual mind is a part of Universal Mind, but is also a whole unto itself. Although both minds are of the same substance – intelligence – they differ significantly in degree. If Universal Mind were an ocean, then individual mind would be a droplet from it.

We are, simultaneously, individual beings with individual mind and universal beings with Universal Mind. The veil of separation is so deceptive that most people have no idea how to access the Universal level of mind.

Individual Mind

Individual mind is the same as local mind. We experience it as the intellect and Ego. We are all intimately familiar with this level of mind. We experience it as our objective, rational mind and our everyday awareness. The instinctual priorities of this level of mind are self-preservation and reproduction.

The intellect is constrained within the rules of logic and reason. That is to say, it is limited to thinking in parts. Its expertise is in breaking down wholes into parts to see how they interact. The study of cause and effect relationships, analysis and scientific inquiry are all hallmarks of the intellect.

The most interesting thing about this level of mind is that it gives birth to the Ego. Its function is to keep us separate from everything else, or individualized, and is a vital part of our functioning. Because of this, the Ego cannot see beyond itself to the next level of wholeness. That is because no holon can see beyond its own level of wholeness. Thus, it can never perceive the Universal Mind directly. Only by suppressing the Ego and intellect can one glimpse beyond the separation and fragmentation to the Universal Mind.

Universal Mind

The Universal Mind is non-local and atemporal, meaning it is unbounded and independent of time. The hallmark of this level of mind is creative intelligence, which makes it the most profound phenomenon in the Universe. It is the creative powerhouse behind the design of all of nature and life. This intelligence translates DNA into living things, transmutes elements in stars and caterpillars into butterflies.

The big secret of the ages is that you have access to this intelligence. However, it is not obvious because this access is necessarily indirect. The reason is that direct exposure would overwhelm the intellect in a flash. Nevertheless, through your Inner Power you can tap into it.

We experience the Universal Mind subjectively as intuitive impulses, guidance and inspiration. It resides in the domain of the Higher Self. Its thrusts are growth and expression. The intelligence at this level of mind is unbounded, holistic and contextual.

Unlike our intellect, which is bound to think in parts, the Universal Mind has the capacity to think in wholes and has a direct connection to the fertile grounds of causality itself, Pure Awareness. It does not need to pull anything apart to understand it – it knows precisely how everything affects everything else. Creativity and self-expression are the hallmarks of this intelligence.

The Universal Mind encompasses the same intelligence that gives the perfect expression of seeds into sunflowers. It effortlessly translates the coded sequences within DNA into the vast array of life. It turns thoughts into things in a creative way.

Pure Awareness

In the science of metaphysics, Pure Awareness is also referred to as First Cause, The Absolute, The Light or Universal Consciousness. Whatever you call it, it is the silent observer of all things, physical and metaphysical. The key feature of Pure Awareness is that it is the level of metaphysical causality.

Everything else in the realm of mind is simply an effect of this vast, unbounded and infinitely intelligent awareness.

Its role in the structure of mind is a special one. If letters on a page represented mind, Pure Awareness would be the paper upon which they are printed. It embraces and includes all levels of mind. Its thrust is transcendence: to go beyond what went before. It is the conductor of the symphony of the Universe.

In the next part, you will learn about the building blocks of your Inner Power, how to tap into the intelligence of the Universal Mind and finally a powerful method for accessing Pure Awareness itself.

PART II

HARNESSING YOUR INNER POWER

ELEMENTS OF INNER POWER – UNIVERSAL LAW –
INTENTION – INTUITION – IMAGINATION –
THE PHILOSOPHERS STONE

Chapter Three

Elements of Inner Power

Our deepest fear is not that we are inadequate.
Our deepest fear is that we are powerful beyond measure.
Our light, not our darkness, frightens us most.

- Marianne Williamson

In this part, you will learn about the four elements that make up your Inner Power:

- ✧ Intention
- ✧ Intuition
- ✧ Imagination
- ✧ The Philosopher's Stone

Through your Inner Power, you can summon and command the vast intelligence of the metaphysical Universe. Understanding these elements is the first step to becoming an alchemist and a potent creative force in your own life. Later, you will learn how to apply them to a process called 'manifesting'. So what is manifesting?

Manifesting is the process of projecting things from the metaphysical world into the physical word. To manifest is to transmute thoughts into things, to bring your intentions into reality. Manifesting is the most important skill for an alchemist, and you must master it to turn your life's lead into gold and create tremendous abundance in your life.

The important thing to know about manifesting is that there are immutable laws that govern the process. These laws do not work for some and not for others. In most cases, the cause of failure is ignorance of the underlying principles. When have a solid understanding of the underlying principles, you can confidently begin to master the art and science of manifesting. Without this grounding, you may be tempted to quit at the first hint of failure. To be certain, when properly commanded, the governing laws do not and cannot fail.

You can use these skills to create anything you desire in your life experience. It might be purely monetary and material pleasures. It might be to experience a heartfelt desire, or it may even be spiritual exaltation. There are no limits on what you can create with your Inner Power. In Part III, you will use these skills to manifest the Ultimate Intention – your Higher Purpose. There is no alternative to creating more abundance and fulfilment in your life experience than to manifest your life's work. To manifest your life's work, you are going to need money, resources, people and many inspired ideas. Manifesting skills allow you to tap into the creative intelligence of the Universal Mind to summon all of them to you and your cause.

This intelligence will gladly orchestrate the fulfilment of your intentions as effortlessly as it turns gases into gold. Therefore, learning how to impress upon and tune into the subsequent guidance of this intelligence is the key to manifesting. Inner Power holds the keys to doing this, as each element has a different role in accessing, or 'communicating', with the Universal Mind.

In Part IV, you will learn about a powerful five-step method for manifesting, but before we get to that, there are some fundamentals to cover.

Chapter Four

Universal Law

The first step in understanding Inner Power is to understand the principles upon which they operate. There are fundamental laws that govern the way that the Universe operates. This is true along both the physical and metaphysical dimensions. These immutable principles are called Universal Laws. They never break down, take a day off or decide to work for saints and not for sinners.

In the physical realm, we are all familiar with the effects of gravity. It is governed by a Universal Law that Isaac Newton first articulated, which we now refer to as the Universal Law of Gravitation. It is expressed by the following equation:

$$F = G\frac{m_1 m_2}{r^2}$$

The Universal Law of Gravitation

You do not need to understand the details, except to know that this formula describes how the planets in our solar system affect each other gravitationally. From this law, we know that everything with mass attracts everything else with mass through the force of gravity. If you weigh 70kg, it is because you and earth are attracted to each other with the gravitational force of exactly 70kg. It is not your mass that gives you weight, it is the effects of gravity that gives you weight. You weigh nothing in outer space because the effect of gravitation is negligible. There are no exceptions, ever. If a particle has mass it will be subject to the laws that govern gravitation. It is Law.

It is no different in the metaphysical Universe. In spite of what you may hope for, the Universe is perfectly detached. Whether you are nobler or nicer than the next person is of no consequence, because Law governs it. Laws just do their job. Your job is to become aware of them and use them to your advantage. The two most important Laws in the metaphysical Universe are:

1. The Law of Focus
2. The Law of Polarity

THE LAW OF FOCUS

The Law of Focus is the most powerful law in the metaphysical Universe. Within it lies the key to self-transformation and mastery of the art of manifestation. The Law of Focus states that whatever you focus your attention upon expands. That is, you get more of whatever you focus on. The subject of your focus increases and grows and it becomes a bigger part of your overall life experience.

You, and only you, have the power to choose what to focus your attention on. This ability is the most powerful gift you have. Wherever you focus your attention, awareness flows through to cause expansion. It is the nature of awareness to flow into and expand the subject of its focus.

To operate the Law of Focus requires an intensive and deliberate concentration of all of your attention. It involves bringing your attention into a laser-like focus. Upon achieving this focus, whatever you put your attention on constantly for more than two minutes will begin to multiply and expand in awareness. Since you and the entire Universe are essentially Pure Awareness made manifest, it *must* be drawn into your life experience. It operates in accordance with immutable Law.

To clarify the concepts of awareness and focus, consider the following analogy: Imagine it is a pitch-black night and you are in the woods. You are completely ignorant to what is around you and what dangers are lurking. Next, imagine that you turn on a flashlight and focus its light directly ahead of you. In an instant, you can now see a small portion of the woods, while the rest remains shrouded in darkness. It is entirely up to you where you direct the flashlight, and each shift causes your view of the woods to change.

Just like light from a flashlight, awareness 'illuminates' whatever subject it is cast upon. Until something comes into your awareness, you are ignorant of it. Ignorance is darkness, awareness is light and awareness can only flow where you direct the 'flashlight' of attention. You have complete control of where to direct your focus; therefore, you have control of the most powerful law in the metaphysical Universe. You need not take my word for it; prove it to yourself with the following demonstration.

THE LAW OF FOCUS IN ACTION

Pick up a small object in your immediate vicinity, one that you can hold in your hand. Examine it very closely for a full minute. Pay intense attention to the object and all of its intricacies. Feel its texture and temperature. Notice its scent. Next, close your eyes and visualize it in as much detail as you can for another full minute. Make the image more vivid by exaggerating the colours until they are vibrant. Hold the image on the screen of your mind. Now, go about your daily life without giving it another thought. Over the next week, you will experience firsthand the power of this law. It works every time; it never fails.

THE LAW OF POLARITY

The next key Law involves the principle of polarity. Polarity is the manifestation of two opposite or contrasting principles, and is a fundamental property of the Universe. It is found everywhere in nature, from subatomic particles to mind to emotions. It is a consequence of the whole/part structure of the Universe and occurs wherever there is a localization of the non-local, a differentiation of the Universal to the individual.

To understand the principle, consider light. The essence of light is energy. Light is just nature's way of transferring energy. When observed, light behaves as both a wave and a particle. Scientists call this the wave/particle duality as it simultaneously has localized (particle) and distributed (wave) properties. When scientists look at the whole-like nature, it manifests as oscillating sine waves along the electro-magnetic spectrum. When they force it to display its part-like nature, it manifests as discrete packets of energy called photons.

Where there are waves, there are particles, and wherever there are particles, there is polarity. In light, the polarity of a photon is its 'phase'. All particles possess polarity; in atoms, it manifests as electrons and protons, which are polar opposites in electrical charge. Polarity is the glue that holds the atom together; the opposite charges are required to form stable atoms. To give you an idea of what polarity is, look at the following table:

Examples of Polarity	
Active	Passive
Male	Female
Positive	Negative
Proton	Electron
Acid	Alkali
Love	Hate

These polarities are all opposite but complementary. That is, they are interdependent. The Chinese philosophy of Yin and Yang describes this relationship elegantly. The following symbol represents the interplay of these opposing but complementary forces.

The Symbol of Yin and Yang

THE POLARITY OF MIND

Recall that the physical Universe is a mirror image, a projection, of the metaphysical Universe. Therefore, if the physical Universe expresses polarity, it must stem from the metaphysical Universe.

In the realm of mind, the Universal Mind is infinite and the individual mind is finite. In other words, the Universal is non-local and the individual is local. Considering the earlier light analogy, Universal Mind is a wave and individual mind is a particle. Recall that wherever there are particles there is polarity. This polarity expresses in mind as the active and passive principle. The active principle is the intellect, whilst the passive principle is intuition. Let's look at this in more depth now.

The Active Principle

The active principle manifests as the objective mind. Its intelligence expresses through the intellect. It is rational, deductive and analytical in nature. This principle is associated with the active use of mental energy, such as problem solving. Alchemists refer to this principle using the symbols of the King, or Sulphur.

The Passive Principle

The passive principle manifests as the subjective mind. Its intelligence expresses through intuition. It is image driven and non-linear. This principle is associated with being receptive, open and still. In this state, you feel emotion and receive intuitive impulses. The meditative or alpha state of mind is the expression of this principle in mind. Alchemists refer to this principle using the symbols of the Queen, the moon or salt.

To summarize the relationship:

- The **active principle** is tied to your **partness** and manifests as **intellect**
- The **passive principle** is tied to your **wholeness** and manifests as **intuition**

Scientists use the term left-brain and right-brain to describe this polarity. The left-brain is the same as the intellect (the sun) and the right-brain is intuition (the moon). Whatever you call it, it is the Law of Polarity manifesting in mind. The following table shows this dichotomy:

Individual Mind (King/sulphur/sun)	Universal Mind (Queen/salt/moon)
Logical	Intuitive
Sequential	Simultaneous
Analytical	Synthesizing
Rational	Holistic
Objective	Subjective
Detail oriented	'Big Picture' oriented
Fact rules	Imagination rules
Words and language	Symbols and images
Looks at 'parts'	Looks at 'wholes'

The Polarity of Mind

At this point, you should be aware that neither polarity of mind is superior. Rather, the key is to balance and integrate them both, to fuse them. The result is a harmony between partness and wholeness, the local and non-local, the intellect and intuition. Esoteric alchemists depict this harmony between intellect and intuition as a Royal Union between the King and Queen, as shown in the following picture:

The Royal Union between the King and Queen

Learning how to achieve this union is 'secret to the door of the place most high'. You will learn how to do this in Chapter Eight – The Philosopher's Stone. The next step is to learn about each of the elements that make up your Inner Power, and how they leverage The Law of Focus and the Law of Polarity. We begin by looking at the most primal element of Inner Power – Intention.

Chapter Five

INTENTION

Thou shalt decree a thing and it shall be established unto thee, and the light shall shine upon thy ways.
- Job 22:28

The first element of your Inner Power is intent. It is the active principle of mind and resides in the domain of the intellect, or local mind.

When you intend to create something in your life, you experience it as a quality of inner conviction. You have made up your mind, enough is enough, and you are going to achieve the change you desire. This is a highly energetic state of mind, and the very act of intending ignites the engines of deliberate creation. This is because intent summons the creative intelligence and energy required for its own fulfilment.

Formulating intentions are like planting seeds into fertile soil. They already hold all the information required for expression from your mind into the physical Universe. You can intend to lose weight, build a business empire, get a new job or realize your Higher Purpose. Your job is to get clarity about your intent and allow the creative intelligence of the Universe to orchestrate its unfoldment.

The moment you truly intend to create something, you step across the manifestation threshold. You collapse possibilities into a clear and specific ideal of what you intend to create.

You are certain that you are going to have it and nothing is going to stop you! In this state, you have the mental, emotional and physical energy required to break through natural resistance and begin the manifesting process.

Intention derives its power from The Law of Focus by drawing your mental energy into a focused and coherent beam of intention. Thus, a one-pointed, highly focused intention is the most powerful force in the Universe.

Intent forces your awareness upon what you intend to create and shifts it away from what you do not want. The Law of Focus is always operating to give you more of what you are focusing upon, to compel them into being.

Apart from activating The Law of Focus, intention serves another important function. It unites the three pillars of manifestation into a congruent force. These three pillars are desire, belief and expectancy. That is, you desire it, you believe you can have it and you expect to get it. The following diagram shows this relationship:

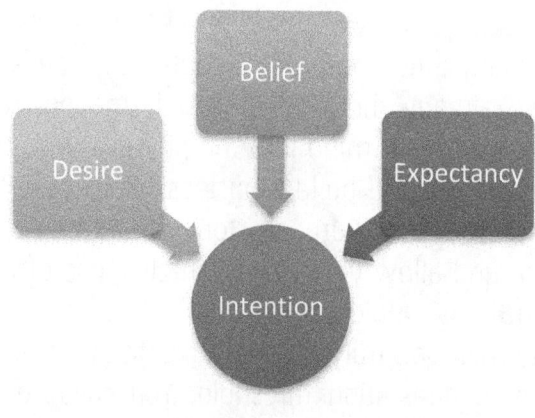

Levels of Intent

Broadly, you can think of any intention as serving one of the following levels of your Being:

Physical
Level: Body
Driver: Survival and reproductive instincts
Manifestations: Food, shelter and sex

Lower Self
Level: Egoic (individual awareness)
Driver: Self-interest and material desires
Manifestations: Self-esteem, self-gratification, self-image, power and social acceptance

Higher Self
Level: Spiritual Self (universal awareness)
Driver: Growth, self-expression and transformation
Manifestations: Higher Purpose, creative expression through unique talents and service to others

Generally, a person will only seek to manifest intentions at their own level of psycho-spiritual development. If a person is highly identified with their Egoic Self, they may not even be conscious of the demands of the Higher Self.

The key to transformational intentions, which hold the most manifesting power, are those intentions aligned with the Higher Self. To actualize your Higher Purpose is the Ultimate Intention, which we will cover in more detail later. You can manifest physical and Egoic intentions effortlessly when your overarching intentions are in alignment with your Higher Self, your Truth.

Divine Intentions

Intentions that seek to serve your Higher Self are Divine Intentions. They transcend your fragmented Ego and seek to serve others, to grow and to transform. These intentions are inspired and infused with Spirit and manifest effortlessly because they add so much value to everyone affected.

When manifesting Divine Intentions, you will herald support from everywhere because others will want to help you realize them. People will be conduits through which the support from the Universe will flow. Synchronicity, life-changing 'lucky' encounters and financial windfalls are part of the everyday experience of someone fulfilling intentions aligned with their Higher Self.

There is a litmus test to determine the integrity of Divine Intentions. Simply ask yourself, does my intention seek to:

- Create value, joy or fulfilment in my life experience,

    AND

- Create value, joy or fulfilment in the lives of others?

Chapter Six

INTUITION

Intuition is the clear conception of the whole at once.
- Johann Kaspar Lavater

Albert Einstein once remarked that 'the only real valuable thing is intuition'. Here is a person who fathered a new paradigm of thought about space and time, and gave us a deeper understanding of the Universe. It is unusual to hear a physical Universe scientist proclaiming the virtues of intuition. But then again, he was no ordinary scientist. It is clear to everyone who understands his work that he was tuned in to something extraordinary. It is just as clear he had mastered the harmony of the two phases of mind, his intellect and intuition.

Unlike intention, intuition does not involve the use of reason or intellect. Intuition is simply a 'knowing' without reason. It is the passive principle of mind and resides in the domain of the Higher Self, or Universal Mind.

The very notion of intuition can stimulate a fiery response from the intellect. Bound by logic, its only conclusion is that a knowing without reason is impossible. The intellect simply cannot grasp it directly, and it never will.

Intuition and the Universal Mind

So what then is all this fuss about intuition? Was Einstein embellishing when he said it was the only real valuable thing? After all, you have travelled along just fine for decades without paying any attention to intuition. Right?

Well, the secret to manifesting is to realize there is a vast and unbounded intelligence behind the world of form. It effortlessly orchestrates the chain of events required to transform exploding stars into everything you see around you now. Everything! Moreover, it is trying to communicate with you right now; it wants to express through you, to become more than it was yesterday, through you. And it is doing all of this through the passive polarity of mind – your intuition.

Even though we experience our everyday reality from the perspective of individual mind, intuition opens the way to the Universal. Through intuition, you can connect to the wholeness far beyond the veils of separation, beyond your fragmented Ego. As you progress along the journey of realizing your Higher Purpose, you will learn that intuition is the key to illuminating your path. Without intuition, your life will continue as a drawn out battle of the intellect, of trial and error, of second-guessing and merely hoping you are on the right path.

Expressions of Intuition

Intuition expresses through awareness in a variety of ways, including:

- ✦ Flash of insight
- ✦ Urge or Impulse
- ✦ Epiphany
- ✦ Inner knowing
- ✦ Gut feeling
- ✦ Revelation
- ✦ Hunch
- ✦ Aha or Eureka! moment

Considering this list, it is clear that intuition is far removed from the domain of reason. We have all had experiences of intuitive guidance, but many people are reluctant to call it such. That is because we have such highly developed reason-based intellects. This basis of thought effortlessly dismisses intuition with its seemingly infallible logic. That is because the intellect is merely doing what it does best – reasoning.

The intellect cannot fathom it let alone understand the mechanism by which it could possibly work, so it concludes it does not exist. However, do not allow its powerful reasoning abilities to confound you. Like an addict, the rational mind is in denial. While it can see the evidence and effects of intuition everywhere, it cannot come to terms with it.

You will notice that you can group the above list into two broad categories. One relates to flashes of thought, the other to feelings. We are going to refer to these as creative and spontaneous intuition, respectively. To help clarify this distinction, study the following diagram for a moment and try to discern the differences for yourself:

Creative Intuition
- Flash of insight
- Aha or Eureka! moment
- Inspiration

Spontaneous Intuition
- Impulse or urge
- Inner knowing
- Gut feeling or hunch

CREATIVE INTUITION

Creative intuition is just what it sounds like. Whether it is a perfect solution, profound insight or just a new way of looking at something, it smacks of 'creativity'. That is, it is a novel way of looking at things that surmounts all the issues or explains all the results. It often involves recognizing new connections between existing knowledge. The flashes are very sharp and clear, they cut through the fog of confusion – you see the way! You will have clarity and a sense of elation and excitement.

In most cases, creative intuition comes after you have applied your intellect intensively to a problem or question. Later on, the answer 'pops' into your head or 'flashes' across your mind. Most stories behind great discoveries share this pattern of intellectual intensity followed by a revelation. These two features are the cornerstones of creative intuition. In the manifesting process, it is intention that focuses the intellect.

So what is happening here? Deep below the horizon of your conscious awareness, ideas are bubbling, coupling, synchronizing and preparing for birth into your awareness. Once synthesized, the Universal Mind expresses the solution to you through intuition.

Your intellect might be protesting at this thought; it would no doubt like to take credit for your magnificent insight. It is probably even dismissing the possibility of Divine Inspiration altogether. Well, how about you stop and ask your intellect if it knows how stardust transmutes into the unimaginably sophisticated brain in which it now resides. Any answer? Enough said!

When you receive intuitive guidance, you will always have your intellect suppressed; you could be walking in nature, taking a shower or even meditating. Archimedes had his famous Eureka! moment while he was having a bath. You never know when or where the creative inspiration comes, it just 'comes from nowhere'. It might take an hour, a day or weeks, you never know.

Spontaneous Intuition

Spontaneous intuition is your everyday intuition. It works much differently to creative intuition. It manifests as the impulses, urges and attraction that you feel toward people, ideas and events. It is clearest when you have a tranquil and clear mental space. Unlike creative intuition, it is faint and subtle. Some common examples of spontaneous intuition are:

- ❖ Knowing who is calling you before you answer
- ❖ An urge to take a different route than normal

- A bad feeling about someone
- A sense of certainty in your next course of action

There is another important distinction between creative and spontaneous intuition. That is, how it flows into your awareness. Intuitive guidance can flow into your awareness in three ways, as shown in the following diagram:

Physical Body - Spontaneous Intuition
- Gut feeling, expansive or contractive physical response
- Very subtle, can be as faint as a whisper

Emotional Body - Spontaneous Intuition
- Feeling, impulse or urge
- Subtle, requires a tranquil mind

Mental Body - Creative Intuition
- Flash of insight, Aha! moment, revelation, epiphany
- Clear and decisive, unmistakeable

Notice that clarity and strength of the intuitive message is lowest in the physical body and highest in the mental body. Flashes of insight hit you like a lightning bolt, whereas a gut feeling radiates gently from within. In addition, notice that the mental body corresponds with creative intuition, while the emotional and physical body corresponds with spontaneous intuition.

Developing both of these types of intuition is important for your growth along the path of mastering the art of manifesting. The key to receiving the guidance offered through intuition is to become receptive to it. The Alchemists Toolkit at the end of this book is devoted to teaching you some simple techniques to become highly receptive to intuitive guidance. I recommend that you turn to it now and familiarize yourself with them before continuing.

Channelling Spontaneous Intuition

A powerful method for channelling spontaneous intuition is with the coin flip technique. Take a coin and assign a yes/no outcome to either heads or tails. Ask yourself a question that is genuinely important to you. Flip the coin to reveal either heads or tails. When you see the outcome, pay close attention to your spontaneous feeling in the instant you see the result. If you feel a sense of expansiveness or relief, then taking action to realize that outcome is in alignment with your Higher Self. If you feel contracted or disappointed, then that outcome does not align with your Higher Self. The key is to disregard your intellect altogether, go with your spontaneous feeling about the result. Your intellect will only serve to inform you of everything that could go wrong. It is trying to protect you from harm, not help you to grow into the magnificent creative force that you are capable of becoming.

Chapter Seven

Imagination

*The imagination is never governed,
it is always the ruling and divine power.*
- John Ruskin

The imagination is your most powerful manifesting tool. Learning how to harness it is the secret to unlocking the real power of intention and intuition. Before you learn how to command its unbounded energy-forming power, you need to understand some basics. In this chapter, you will learn about its role and active and passive polarities.

The role of imagination is to act as the gateway between individual and Universal Mind. The gateway allows intelligence to flow between the finite and the infinite, the local and non-local.

The Master Translator

Earlier we established that you have access to two minds, an individualized mind and Universal Mind. The individual mind is logical, rational and sequential whilst the Universal Mind is intuitive, holistic and simultaneous. Because of this, they both speak entirely different languages. The role of imagination is to act as the intermediary between the individual mind and Universal Mind. Therefore, it must translate the language used to communicate between partness and wholeness. It does this with mental imagery, specifically symbolic imagery.

SYMBOLIC IMAGERY

Have you ever heard the expression 'a picture speaks a thousand words?' This is true; however, this is only half the story. That is because 'a symbol speaks a thousand pictures!'

Throughout the ages, we have used symbols to express ideas and relationships that escape the grasp of words. Symbols capture the subjective essence or quality of something free from the constraints of language.

When you see a symbol, it is up to you to contextualize and interpret it. This occurs within your own framework of associations. You will learn more about this in Part III, but for now, it is enough to know that the imagination translates the intelligence of the Universal into symbols.

THE POLARITY OF IMAGINATION

Mental energy flows constantly between your mind and the Universal Mind. You can shape and form this energy with your imagination. The direction that this energy is flowing determines which polarity of imagination you are using. The flow from:

- ✧ Individual to Universal is **active** imagination.
- ✧ Universal to individual is **passive** imagination.

Active Imagination

You engage the active imagination through *visualization*. Visualization involves deliberately projecting *mental imagery* upon the screen of your mind. The active imagination is the tool you use to shape 'formless substance', which is another term for pure creative potential. You have the power to mould 'formless substance' with your active imagination. Whatever is properly impressed upon 'formless substance' sets the cast for expression into form. You will learn how to do this in step two of the manifesting method, called impression.

Passive Imagination

You engage the passive imagination through *visioning*. Visioning involves interpreting imagery that flows passively onto the screen of your mind. In the passive state of imagination, you are not consciously directing the mental imagery. The passive imagination is the tool you use to receive inspiration and guidance from the Universal. You experience passive imagination every time you dream or fantasize. The images flow effortlessly without any of your own conscious involvement. In the most receptive state of mind, you allow whatever comes into your imagination.

The passive imagination is so ingenious that it will generate symbolic imagery designed especially for you. If you are passionate about chemistry, the imagery might come through your passive imagination as chemicals interacting in a meaningful way. If mathematics is your thing, equations and operators might flash to mind. The point is that symbols are contextual and personalized just for you. They will not mean the same thing to someone else because they have a different set of associations. Let us look at a famous example of the passive imagination in action.

Example of Passive Imagination

In 1864 German chemist, Friedrich Kekule discovered the chemical structure of Benzene. Prior to his discovery, scientists thought that the structure of molecules was linear. However, a linear structure did not explain many of the properties of Benzene. So how did he come to revolutionize the field of organic chemistry? Read his account of the event below:

> "...I was sitting writing on my textbook, but the work did not progress; my thoughts were elsewhere. I turned my chair to the fire and dozed. Again, the atoms were gambolling before my eyes. This time the smaller groups kept modestly in the background. My mental eye, rendered more acute by the repeated visions of the kind, could now distinguish larger structures of manifold conformation; long rows sometimes more closely fitted together all twining and twisting in snake-like motion. But look! What was that? One of the snakes had seized hold of its own tail, and the form whirled mockingly before my eyes. As if by a flash of lightning I awoke; and this time also I spent the rest of the night in working out the consequences of the hypothesis."[1]

---

[1] Royston M. Roberts, Serendipity, Accidental Discoveries in Science, John Wiley and Sons, New York, NY, 1989, pp. 75-81.

This imagery of the snake biting its tail and whirling mockingly at him made him realize that the structure of Benzene was ring-like. Thanks to the power of passive imagination, the rest is history!

ACTIVE-PASSIVE IMAGINATION

Using both the active and passive phases of imagination together is very powerful application of the Law of Polarity. This technique is termed 'active visioning' and it enables you to access the intelligence of the Universal Mind very effectively. In active visioning, you consciously form the initial imagery, but then release it to your passive imagination to mould and shape it in response to a question. You will learn a powerful technique to harness this special use of imagination in Part III.

Chapter Eight

The Philosopher's Stone

In this chapter, you will learn about the history of the fabled Philosopher's Stone. You will also learn the secret of how to forge it for yourself using a simple method.

For centuries, the holy grail of the alchemists' pursuit was to forge 'the stone that is not a stone'. It has been called many things throughout the ages, including the 'pearl of great price', the 'white stone by the river' and the 'sword in the stone'. Although it goes by many names, its sole function has always remained the same. The Philosopher's Stone is a catalyst, said to transmute invaluable lead into valuable gold.

Over the centuries, the search for the Philosopher's Stone has consumed the lives of many, counting Sir Isaac Newton, Carl Jung and St. Thomas Aquinas as members of a fraternity that devoted much of their lives studying alchemy. The pursuit is even purported to have taken the life of Newton, whose body contained massive amounts of mercury due to his alchemical pursuits.

To understand alchemy and the pursuit of The Stone, you must view it from two perspectives. The first view relates to the world without, while the second, to the world within.

The first is the well-known material alchemy. Their quest was to create elemental gold out of base metals, such as lead. The promise of great riches to the alchemist who accomplished this feat lured many into field. However, their quest proved ultimately futile. We now understand that only nuclear reactions within stars or particle accelerators can produce the energy required to transmute elements. However, the science of alchemy does not end there.

The second is esoteric or divine alchemy. The esoteric alchemist's aim was to transmute the base metals of *ignorance* into the gold of *awareness*. The objective was to transmute leaden consciousness into golden consciousness. It was to transmute bondage into freedom and poverty into abundance through a direct rapport with the Higher Self. It was to dissociate from the lower self, the Ego, and associate with the Higher Self, or Spirit. The esoteric alchemists called this shift in identification 'The Great Work'. Therein lays the true gold that the alchemists sought.

As you learn how to command your Inner Power, summon Universal intelligence and use it to realize your Higher Purpose, your awareness grows and you find your gold. When you apply this knowledge in service to others, you create gold in your own life in the form of abundance, prosperity and fulfilment. While this process eventually results in profound self-transformation, it may still take years to unfold.

However, there is a faster way! To accelerate the process of attaining the 'golden consciousness' that unlocks the full might of your Inner Power, requires the presence of a catalyst. The most powerful catalyst in the metaphysical Universe is the Philosopher's Stone. The Stone will accelerate your growth exponentially and grant you access to true power. It also takes a critical role in the manifesting process, which you will learn about in Part III. Before you discover what it is, it helps to understand its alchemical background.

Vitriol

According to medieval alchemists, the key to activating The Philosophers Stone is with a substance they called Vitriol. The word Vitriol derives from the Latin word *vitreus*, meaning glass, referring to the glassy appearance of the sulphate salts. For example, blue vitriol is copper sulphate and green vitriol is iron sulphate. Vitriol was so important to the alchemists because it can dissolve every metal it encounters, except for gold. Gold is the only metal resistant to its highly corrosive action; creating gold was the key objective of the alchemist!

To prepare Vitriol, alchemists would burn sulphur together and saltpetre in the presence of steam. This is why in esoteric alchemy, sulphur represents the active principle and salt represents the passive principle. Through this fusion of the active and passive principles, the alchemist would produce Vitriol. So what is the secret to producing Vitriol and activating The Stone?

The esoteric alchemists hid their secret openly through symbolism and cryptic texts. Only initiates skilled in the art could decipher their meaning. However, 15th century alchemist Basilius Valentinus gives us the secret to forging the stone in his work L'Azoth des Philosophes in plain language. Examine carefully the following emblem, which contains the secret to making The Stone:

Emblem from L'Azoth des Philosophes

Pay particular attention to the wording on the outside of the emblem, which says *Visita Interiora Terræ Rectificando Invenies Occultum Lapidem.* Upon closer inspection, you will notice that it is also an acronym spelling V.I.T.R.I.O.L. This then is the secret formula to producing the esoteric alchemists Vitriol. So what does it mean?

Translated, it simply says 'Visit the interior of the earth and, by purifying it, you will find the hidden stone'. The interior of the earth is a metaphor for consciousness or awareness. So, to forge the stone, you purify your awareness to the point that mind is transcended entirely. Thus, the Philosophers Stone is not a thing, not a stone, but a state of awareness. It is Pure Awareness itself!

When you attain this state of awareness, you transcend the polarity of mind altogether. This state of mind is referred to as cessation, in which mind ceases entirely and you abide in brief windows of Pure Awareness. During these short windows, you can achieve the integration of the part with the whole, the local with the non-local, the finite with the infinite. The contemplative traditions refer to this state of being as Cosmic or Unity Consciousness. You experience the brilliant radiance of your own true nature, Pure Awareness itself. Like Vitriol, Pure Awareness dissolves everything in its presence, except for true gold!

You take the individual, infuse it with the Universal, and take both back to your everyday life. It is the realization of your essential whole/part nature. To produce The Stone is to unite with your wholeness and to open a window to the 'formless substance' of the Universal.

How To Prepare The Philosopher's Stone

To experience the Philosopher's Stone firsthand does not require immersion in ancient alchemical texts or esoteric experiments. You can behold the 'Pearl of Great Price' with an ancient technique called Japa Meditation. It is a powerful and transformational technique. It will take a couple of sessions before you get the hang of it, so be patient with yourself until then.

The easiest way to accomplish this state is to focus all of your attention onto a single focal point. In this case, the most natural sound your vocal chords can produce. It requires only the relaxation of your voice, with only air passing over your vocal chords. It is the ancient sound of 'Ahh'.

The technique is easiest to learn by following guided audio instructions, which you can download free on the website by visiting the resources section. If you would prefer to read the instructions, they are as follows:

FORGING THE STONE TECHNIQUE

1. Get prepared by relaxing with your hands on your hips facing upwards. Lightly press your thumb and forefinger together until they are just touching. Close your eyes
2. Visualise the letter A that almost fills the screen of your imagination for a few moments

3. To the right of the letter, visualize the letter B for a few moments

4. Shift your focus to the 'gap of nothingness' between the two letters, A & B

5. Take a deep luxurious breath that fills your lungs to capacity
6. Say the sound 'Ahh' for as long as you comfortably can until your breath runs out. The key is to concentrate all of your attention upon the sound of 'Ahh'. Hear it in your ears, hear it reverberate around the room, feel it vibrate in your body. If your thoughts wander, gently refocus your attention back on the sound and vibrations
7. Repeat step 6 so that you have done two full breaths making the 'Ahh' sound
8. Shift your focus back to the letter B for a few moments

9. To the right of the letter, visualize the letter C

10. Shift your focus to the space between the two letters, B & C
11. Repeat the 'Ahh' process and continue this pattern until you have done 7-10 letters

The process is gradual, and each repetition will get you closer to The Stone, the state of cessation. After you have practiced the method a few times, you will begin to experience the expansion into wholeness by the 15-minute mark. After 20 minutes, you ought to have fully transcended into Pure Awareness itself, the domain of First Cause. The sharper and more complete your focus is upon the sound to the exclusion of everything else, the more profound your experience will be. After around four exposures to The Stone, you will begin to be able to produce it without going through this full process. You will be able to produce it whenever you are highly relaxed and centred simply by focusing upon the 'Ahh' sound.

Tips For Forging The Stone

- ✧ Guided audio is the best way to learn the technique
- ✧ Practice forging The Stone first thing in the morning or the just before sleep
- ✧ A small amount of alcohol consumed beforehand has the effect of relaxing you further, enhancing the ease of forging The Stone.
- ✧ Conjuring up the emotion of love, joy or gratitude in the last few letters of the cycles supercharges the experience and can results in tears of joy and immense humility.
- ✧ Do not attempt this technique when you are frustrated or tired

In the next part, you will learn how to apply the metaphysical laws, principles and elements of Inner Power within a powerful framework for manifestation.

PART III

THE SCIENCE OF MANIFESTING

FIVE-STEP MANIFESTING METHOD –
INTENTION – IMPRESSION –
SURRENDER – ILLUMINATION – INSPIRED
ACTION

CHAPTER NINE

THE FIVE-STEP MANIFESTING METHOD

Life in itself is an empty canvas;
it becomes whatsoever you paint on it.
You can paint misery, you can paint bliss.
This freedom is your glory.
- Osho

In this chapter, you will learn a five-step method for manifesting. As you have learnt, manifesting is the process of bringing your intentions from your inner world into your outer world, where you can experience them with your physical senses. You can apply this method to manifest any intention, regardless of what level of your being it serves. As you grow in experience, you will grow in mastery. You will begin with small objects or amounts of money, and progress to ever larger and grander intentions. The key to becoming a powerful manifestor is by gaining ever-increasing trust in the process. Eventually, it becomes an unshakeable inner knowing and an integral part of your Being. In Part IV, you will receive practical guidance on how to manifest the Ultimate Intention, your Higher Purpose. The skill of manifesting is easily the most important in realizing your Divine Mission, which is your Higher Purpose made manifest.

To begin, take the time study the following diagram to see how each element of Inner Power relates to one another.

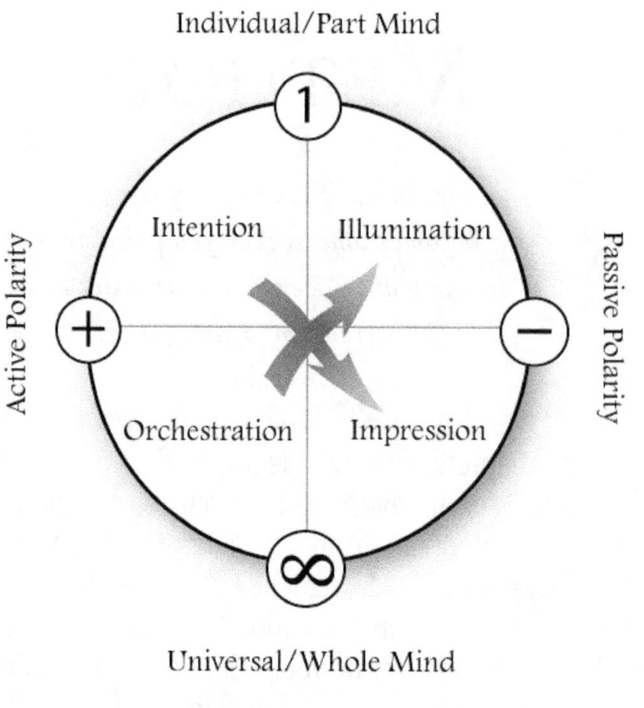

The Metaphysics of Manifestation

The arrows represent the active and passive flow of imagination between individual mind and Universal Mind.

The intention of the individual is impressed upon the Universal with active imagination. In response, the Universal will orchestrate the people, events and resources required for fulfilment. Finally, the Universal Mind will illuminate the path of least action through intuition and the passive imagination.

The five-step manifesting method is based upon the flow of mental energy through the polarities of individual and Universal Mind, as illustrated below:

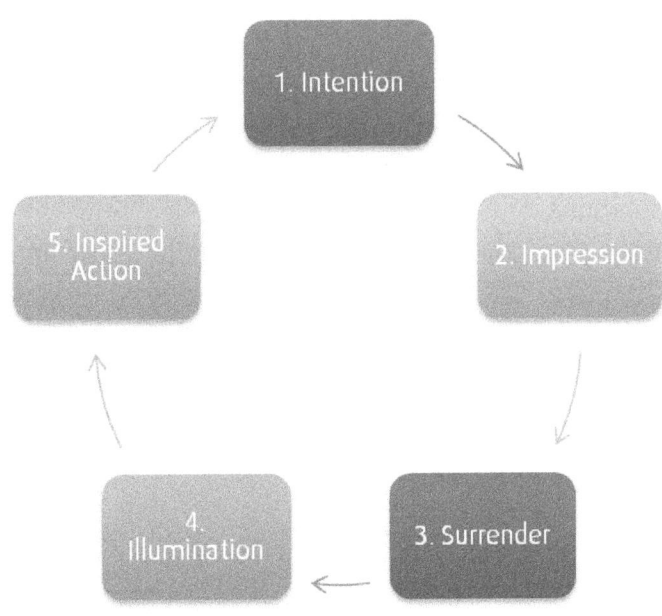

The Five-Step Manifesting Method

Step 1

Intention

As you learnt in Part II, intention activates the Law of Focus. This makes intent the most powerful force in the metaphysical Universe. To command intent, you must first clearly articulate exactly what it is you intend to create. In this book, the focus is upon the actualization of your Higher Purpose to create abundance. However, you can use this formula to articulate any intention.

When formulating your intentions, it is important not to focus on how you are going to manifest them. You are not to concern yourself with how or when it will happen. The details will unfold in the illumination stage, and you will have your clarity about the actions to take then. Your job is to decide upon what you intend to create, get clarity about it and then impress it upon the Universal. Your first step is to get your intention into a workable form.

The Intent Decree

The most effective way to express an intention is with an Intent Decree. An Intent Decree is a brief statement that expresses, in powerful language, what you intend to create and why. They are comprised of three simple statements, shown as follows:

I **intend** to …
I **am** …
I **love** …

Element 1: I intend to …

Here you state what you intend to achieve and how you intend to feel when your intention has manifested.

I intend to … (do)
I intend to … (feel)

For example:

- ✧ I intend to identify my Higher Purpose and act to realize it
- ✧ I intend to feel a sense of meaning and fulfilment in my life experience

Element 2: I am …

The key to creating compelling 'I am…' statements is to ensure they are true for you. Forget what you have learnt about affirmations that suggest you lie to yourself. You expect other people to tell you the truth, so tell yourself the truth. There are much more effective ways of transforming limiting beliefs than through self-deceptive autosuggestion.

Besides, it is easy to tell yourself the truth with 'I am...' statements. You need only preface them all with the words:

I am *now in the process of* ...

For example, you could preface the following statements with 'I am now in the process of':

- ✧ Realizing my Higher Purpose
- ✧ Becoming a millionaire
- ✧ Achieving my ideal weight
- ✧ Creating more abundance
- ✧ Expanding my business
- ✧ Attracting my soul mate

There is no dissonance in your mind when you say these statements. They are expansive truths, not contractive lies. Most importantly, they help to evoke the feeling of having what you want, not the lack of it.

Element 3: I love ...

Love is a very powerful word. When you say you love something, you charge the subject with the vitality of love. You can use the following opening statements to express your love for the subject of your intent:

I love **how it feels to** ...
I love **the idea of** ...
I love **seeing myself** ...

For example:

- ✧ I love how it feels to live my life on purpose and have others tell me what an impact my work has on them
- ✧ I love the idea of being a world-renowned transformational speaker
- ✧ I love seeing myself in front of a captivated audience who enjoy my lectures

To summarize, the formula for constructing an intent decree is as follows:

I intend to ... (do)
I intend to ... (feel)
I am now in the process of ...
I love how it feels/the idea of/seeing myself ...

Once you have each of the elements of your Intent Decree, it is simply a matter of stringing them together. Here is an example:

INTENT DECREE FOR HIGHER PURPOSE

I intend to identify my Higher Purpose and act to realize it. I intend to feel abundant and fulfilled as a result. I am now in the process of creating tremendous abundance by serving others with my passions. I love how it feels to live my life on purpose and serve others with my special talents.

Intent Decree Worksheet

I intend to ... (do)
_____
_____
_____

I intend to ... (feel)
_____
_____
_____

I am now in the process of ...
_____
_____
_____

I love how it feels/the idea of/seeing myself ...
_____
_____
_____

Intent Decree for _____

_____
_____
_____
_____
_____

Step 2

Impression

Impression is the act of moulding the 'formless substance' of Universal Mind with intent. Your active imagination is the most effective means to accomplish this. Essentially, you visualize your fulfilled intention in the presence of The Stone.

The first step is to translate your Intent Decree into imagery. When vitalized with gratitude, the highest energy emotion, this imagery sets the cast for the creative intelligence of the Universal to flow into for expression.

Impression causes tremendous tension in the structure of consciousness. This is because impression creates incongruence between the vitalized imagery and actual reality. The mind cannot long tolerate this contrast between what is impressed and what is experienced. The world without must correspond to the world within, just as expression must correspond to impression. The Universe will seek to close the gap and resolve the tension to restore equilibrium. The physical Universe always seeks its lowest energy state, and the metaphysical Universe is no different.

The Universal, simultaneously connected to everyone and everything conscious, will seek the path of least resistance to resolve this tension. It does this by matching your intention with the intentions of others that align with it. They will help you fulfil your intention and you will help fulfil theirs. You will find yourself giving in ways you ordinarily would not. You will resonate strongly with causes, people, ideas and events that had no significance in the past. You will also notice the sudden appearance of amazing coincidences.

The Universe is the ultimate utilitarian, which means it will always seek the greatest good for the most people. This is the reason why Divine Intentions are so powerful. The entire Universe literally lines up behind you, supporting you through its vast armies of angels who, just like you, want to serve the greater good. Everybody wins, especially your Higher Self, which is in it for growth, expression and the creation of tremendous value for others.

Relative Impression Power

A key objective of the manifestation method is to impress your intention upon the Universal Mind, with the belief and knowing that your intention has already manifested. It is a critical step in the process, and all subsequent steps will falter if the impression is inadequate. Therefore, it is crucial that the most powerful impression techniques are used.

The following table shows the relative impression power of a variety of techniques:

Power	Impression Method
1	One-off thought
2	One-off written word
3	One-off verbalization
4	One-off visual imagery
10	Repeated thought
20	Repeated written word
30	Repeated verbalization
40	Repeated visual imagery
70	Emotionally charged thought
80	Emotionally charged written word
90	Emotionally charged verbalization
100	Emotionally charged visual imagery
1000	Emotionally charged visual imagery in the presence of The Stone

Notice from this list that the power increases through thought, word, verbalization, and imagery. You will also note that repetition adds power, but endless repetition of words cannot overpower even a single highly emotionalized thought impulse.

For our purposes, what we are interested in is only the most powerful method. This is the last one on the list, with a relative power of 1,000. It is orders of magnitude more powerful than repeated affirmations. This is because you transcend mind entirely and penetrate directly into the realm of Pure Awareness, or First Cause. This level of awareness is the causal level of the metaphysical Universe. Everything else is an effect operating in a direct causal response to this super-conscious level. At this level of awareness, you can recast fundamental beliefs and undo years of negative programming in moments. The vitriolic power of The Stone dissolves all untruth and negativity within its presence. The only thing left untouched is the gold of awareness and the realization of The Truth.

IMPRESSING FORMLESS SUBSTANCE

There are three elements to impressing formless substance:

1. Visual imagery
2. Emotional charge
3. The Philosophers Stone

We shall look at each in detail before tackling the practical aspects of the method.

1. VISUAL IMAGERY

You learnt in Part II that the imagination is the gateway between the individual and Universal. So then, the first step involves translating your intent decree into both *literal* and *symbolic* imagery. So what is the difference between the two?

LITERAL IMAGERY

Literal imagery is a visual scenario of what your fulfilled intention will look like. Think of it as painting the Universe a picture of what you want. The crucial point to note is that you must use only imagery of what your fully realized intention will look like. For instance, if your intention is attract a large sum of money in to your life, you could visualize a bank statement showing a balance of $100,000.

Bear in mind that you must not use imagery that tries to show how you would go about creating or finding this money, such as winning a lottery or starting up a business. Your job at this stage is simply to paint the picture, to make the impression, to see only the result.

Ensure that your scenario is from a first-person perspective, looking out through your own eyes. If your intention is to manifest a brand new car, go to a showroom and experience sitting in the driver's seat. Notice the colour of the leather and wood grain, and the layout of the instruments. The more detail you can paint in your picture, the better. The key is to make the imagery as vivid as possible, so it is best that you experience it first-hand before formulating your imagery.

Symbolic Imagery

Symbolic imagery captures the subjective essence of the fulfilled intention. Recall that the Universal uses symbols to express its intelligence to your finite mind through passive imagination. But, it is a two way street, and you can use symbols to communicate the subjective qualities of your fulfilled intention directly to the Universal.

To give you a better idea, consider the following two examples of symbols that I use personally. Bear in mind that because symbols are personal and contextual, they are not likely to evoke the same associations for you.

A Frangipani Flower

For me, the symbol of the frangipani flower represents simplicity and abundance. They are simple yet strikingly beautiful, and remind me that beauty and harmony stem from simplicity. I have the association with abundance because I would pick a few of the flowers everyday to decorate my workspace over an entire summer. It did not matter how many I picked, there always seemed to be a never-ending supply of them. After a few weeks, every time I picked one I would feel the subjective essence of abundance. One of my favourite Upanishads quote would come to mind and I would find myself quoting: *'From abundance I took abundance and still abundance remained'*.

A Glass Prism

For me, the prism symbolises imagination and creative expression. It is symbolic of the bridge between the part and the whole, the local and the non-local. That is because the white light and the full colour spectrum of which it is comprised is revealed though it. It takes the whole and breaks it down into parts. It inspires me to think of ways to turn apparently boring 'white light' situations into creative expressions that give rise to joy and fulfilment.

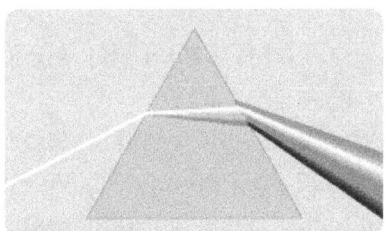

It is important to understand that at the back of all intentions is a feeling, an emotional charge. That is, you are intending to *feel* some quality or emotion when your intention manifests, such as:

Power	Freedom	Love
Respect	Acceptance	Comfort
Confidence	Belonging	Joy
Growth	Accomplishment	Grace
Youthfulness	Sex Appeal	Success

Your task is to find a symbol that encapsulates whichever feeling or subjective quality is at the heart of your intention. If a symbol is not immediately apparent, you can enlist the power of your passive imagination.

To do this, get quiet, close your eyes, and clear the screen of your imagination. Ask yourself 'which symbol represents the quality of ____ for me?' Just be receptive to whatever images flow across your mind. Choose the one that evokes the most feeling for you, the one you resonate with the most. When you have selected your symbol, immerse yourself in it. Find some pictures of it or get the actual object itself. Hang it up for display in your room, at work and in the bathroom.

2. Emotional Charge

Emotional energy is the workhorse of the impression process. Although the imagery and active visualization process provides the Universe with an outline for the impression, emotional energy is what causes the extrusion of 'formless substance' into form.

To understand why, you need to think of emotions as being energy in the metaphysical Universe. Since light is the transporter of energy in the physical Universe, it is a useful analogy. In the physical Universe, we perceive the highest vibration (frequency) light as the colour violet and the lowest vibration light as the colour red. In fact, the electromagnetic waves of violet light vibrate 320 trillion times a second faster than red light.

The same idea applies to emotions, so we have high energy and low energy emotions. So, in this analogy, you can think of each emotion as a different 'colour', depending on its energy level, or vibration. This following table shows how each colour corresponds with emotional energy:

Vibration	Emotion
Violet	Gratitude, love, joy
Indigo	Passion, enthusiasm
Blue	Hope, optimism
Green	Contentment, satisfaction
Yellow	Doubt, frustration
Orange	Worry, blame, anger
Red	Despair, hatred, depression

From this table we see that gratitude, love and joy are of the highest vibration. They have a profound transformative power over everything they encounter. On the other hand, the lowest vibration emotions such as despair and hatred are destructive and repressive.

The key is to understand that higher vibration emotions have more energy. The hottest visible flames are violet and the coldest flames are red, because violet flames require much more energy than red ones to generate.

To create this energy requires deliberate and conscious effort. To generate gratitude or joy you must deliberately focus your awareness upon the things for which you are grateful for or that bring you joy. On the other hand, you can produce worry and despair effortlessly. They are like the default ground state; it is easier to let depression overwhelm you than to rise to joy. So what is the single most powerful emotion you can use to impress upon the Universal?

Gratitude

By far, the most powerful energy is contained within the emotion of gratitude. It is the master manifesting emotion and you must employ it to do the real work of impressing 'formless substance'.

The emotion of gratitude also serves another important function, which is to cause you to feel that your intention has already manifested; not tomorrow, not on your next payday, not when you win the lottery, right now! When you are expressing gratitude, you are emotionalizing the intent as though you already have it. This feeling of having it now is a key element of the process, and expressing gratitude for it even though you do not yet have it is essential. So how can you generate the feelings of gratitude?

Summoning gratitude is easy when you engage the most powerful law in the metaphysical Universe – The Law of Focus. You need only commit to focusing on what you are grateful for instead of what is missing in your life. The most effective way to do this is to start a gratitude journal. A gratitude journal is simply a diary that you write in at the end of each day. In it, you express all of the things you are grateful for throughout the day. Its simplicity belies its tremendous power in lifting your energy to the violet end of the emotional spectrum. The energy and effort you spend on your gratitude journal will pay you tremendous dividends. Commit to devoting five minutes each night before you retire to your gratitude journal.

3. The Philosophers Stone

Using visualization and gratitude alone is a powerful method for impression; however, to obtain truly profound results requires the presence of a catalyst. As you learnt in Part II, the most powerful catalyst in the metaphysical Universe is The Stone. The Stone is a metaphor for Pure Awareness, or First Cause. In this state of awareness, you literally transcend your individual mind and shift into the *causal level* of the metaphysical Universe.

Perform this method first thing in the morning or before retiring. It takes only twenty minutes, and you only ever need do it once for each intention. When properly moulded, 'formless substance' simply does not forget!

1. Firstly, spend five minutes writing in your gratitude journal and give thanks for all that you are grateful.
2. Next, write out your Intent Decree in your gratitude journal.
3. Sketch a picture or close your eyes and imagine what your fulfilled intention will look like. Remember to stay in the first-person perspective.
4. Get quiet, close your eyes and perform The Stone Technique until you are experiencing it fully. This will take around fifteen minutes or ten-letter transitions in most cases.
5. At this point, forget about the letters completely.
6. While continuing to repeat the mantra, project a snapshot of your fulfilled intention onto the screen of your imagination. After three or four repetitions of the

mantra, allow silence to pass while you continue to project the imagery.
7. The last step is to attach the emotion of gratitude to your imagery, while continuing to repeat the mantra. This is when the real magic happens. The feeling of gratitude should still be fresh in your awareness. Emotionalize your imagery by immersing yourself in overwhelming thanks as if it was now a reality.

If you have followed these instructions, rest assured that you have impressed your intent upon 'formless substance'. You have completed your role in the active phase of the manifesting process; the Universe will orchestrate the means for fulfilment and expression into form.

STEP 3

SURRENDER

It is time to sit back and relax! You must now release your intention into the hands of the Universe. You must let it go altogether and go about your daily business. The act of surrender is about releasing your lower self's grip on the intention. It is about detaching from the outcome and trusting in the Universe to orchestrate fulfilment.

The secret to effective surrender is to have a playful, child-like knowing that it will express in its own perfect time. You do not know, or want to know how, nor should you care. Just leave it up to the Universe to handle all the details. You must release to receive, and this is usually the most difficult step for apprentice alchemists.

The other essential aspect of surrender is to let go of any desperation or neediness of having your intention fulfilled. This is because being receptive to intuitive guidance is an essential part of the process. It is a direct conduit to wholeness, your Higher Self, and the unbounded orchestrating intelligence of the Universal Mind. Nevertheless, it is a passive channel, and the active nature of the intellect will always over-rule it in times of need and desperation.

When you surrender fully, you disengage the intellect and allow fulfilment to express in ways your intellect cannot possibly conceive. Remember the intellect is anchored within the individual mind with no direct rapport with the Universal Mind. Because of this fragmentation and isolation, it is the cause of all resistance to complete surrender.

PATIENCE

Can you remember a situation where you really lost your patience? Chances are that the outcome was not a positive one. It is not always easy to remain patient throughout the manifesting process, especially if you have put a lot of money, time or energy into manifesting an intention. Nevertheless, you will need to transcend the temptation to rush the manifestation process. The entire method will falter quickly in the presence of impatience, frustration and ego-driven demands for faster results.

Impatience and excessive attachment to the outcome are long time bedfellows. Both cause feelings of frustration and despair, which are very low vibration emotions and have no place in the manifesting process. To stay in the frictionless flow, you must act quickly to re-focus your attention and increase the energy in your emotions to joy and gratitude. Inspiration will express itself more clearly and frequently in the presence of high vibration thought and emotion. When your overall emotional vibrations drop down into this range, you lose your connection with Universal intelligence. If there is no action in joy, surrender and gratitude then there is no inspiration. Without inspiration, there is no effortless ease, no grace and no synchronicity.

On your path to mastery of the manifesting method, you will learn to exercise Infinite Patience. Infinite Patience is an inner knowing that there is a season for all things, and that everything comes in its own good time. This perspective can only come from experience in the process. Eventually, you will have accumulated so much evidence that you will begin to trust that this process works. You will reason that because all of your past intentions have been actualized, so too will all of your current and future intentions.

The big secret is that, paradoxically, the more patient you are the faster your intentions will manifest. That is because the state of Infinite Patience fosters surrender and expectancy.

Expectancy

Patience and expectancy are complementary states of mind. Expectancy is active in nature, such that you are actively looking forward to your intention manifesting. Patience is more passive, in that you are in no hurry for it to come but you know that it will. Expectancy will push and patience will pull you along the path to the realization of your intention. Maintaining a harmony between patience and expectancy is critical to the process.

You might recall from Part II that expectancy is one of the three elements of Intention, alongside desire and belief. Anything you can do to reinforce your expectancy will greatly increase the fluidity and speed of the manifesting process.

When you expect money, a resource, or even inspiration to come to you, it sends a very clear signal to the Universe. The important thing to remember with expectancy is that you will not get the money, resource or idea until the exact time that it is required. For that reason, you must not lose faith in your expectancy at the last minute. Many people prematurely abort the process because what they are expecting to support them has not shown up well in advance.

The Universe is a highly efficient operation and it is perfectly reliable. It is the Ego, your partness, which demands the security of all the resources in advance. That is fair enough, the Ego's drive is toward self-preservation and protection. It would not be doing its job if it exposed you to unnecessary risk. Nevertheless, you must recognize that it cannot comprehend the ways your Higher Self will support you at the perfect moment, when you trust in it. Allow grace, synchronicity and effortless ease to propel you along the path toward realization. Your job is to over-rule the demands of your Ego by out-picturing with your unwavering expectancy.

For example, say you require a certain sum of money by a certain time, but there is no sign of it and the deadline is approaching. Your intellect will cause you to become anxious about the fact that you do not already have the money well in advance. The intellect reasons, 'Oh Universe, why can't I have it now so I can sleep soundly at night?' Unfortunately, for the intellect, the Universe does not operate that way. If you have impressed upon 'formless substance' and keep yourself anchored in the high of the emotional spectrum, and expect the money, you will get it! It will come not a moment too soon, or a moment too late. The unbounded orchestrating intelligence will deliver it right on time! Your job is to keep your faith in the process and expect it to be there when it is required.

Faith

This kind of expectancy is the essence of true faith, or trust, in the Universe. Your intellect will never allow this degree of trust until you have built it up one-step at a time. Knowing this, you can start by manifesting small things, growing in trust until you build an unshakeable inner knowing. The evidence will just keep piling up until your intellect can no longer deny the truth. Once this happens, you can truly surrender your lower self to your Higher Self, and your manifesting ability will grow exponentially. You can read entire bookshelves about this faith or trust, and about other people's success with it. However, until you have proven it to the only person who matters, yourself, it has no constructive power in the process.

You will have plenty of opportunities to fully develop this faith, but extend it a little trust to begin with and work from there. Rest assured, the same intelligence that transformed you from a few strands of DNA could not let you down if it wanted to. It operates to give expression to your impression in accordance with perfect law; it knows no failure. Follow the five-step manifestation process outlined in this book and the Universe will support you.

Step 4

Illumination

*Intuition is a spiritual faculty and does not explain,
but simply points the way.*
- Florence Scovel Shinn

Up to this point, you have impressed your intention upon 'formless substance' and surrendered it to the Universe. As a direct causal consequence, the same creative intelligence that transforms stardust into life has been working for you behind the scenes. Having orchestrated all of the details necessary for fulfilment, Universal Intelligence will seek to express the means for expression through your intuition. Illumination is the result of this intuitive guidance entering into your awareness. There are two ways that you can receive illumination. The first pathway is passive, while the other is active.

Passive Illumination

Passive illumination is the same as creative intuition, or Divine Inspiration. This type of illuminating guidance will come to you as a revelation or flash of insight. In other cases, it will come from a cue in your environment. It might be something someone says to you or a significant sign along your path.

Passive illumination can take anywhere from a day to a month to express, and you have no control over the timing of it. Your only role in this passive process is to be receptive to intuitive guidance.

Nonetheless, this illumination is usually unmistakeable. This is because the answer will literally jump out at you. Things that you would not have given a second thought to will suddenly stand out as if put there just for you, and it will emanate a feeling of importance. Moreover, you will feel clarity, excitement and enthusiasm about taking action on the inspiration. Dismissal of this illumination further provokes its frequency, urging you toward action.

The key is to resist intellectualizing these intuitive signals and just flow with them. Your intellect will only interfere as it tries in vain to comprehend their significance. The manifesting process is not a rational or linear one. Rather, it is non-linear and holistic. Because your intellect is bound to linearity, it will try to dismiss the appearance of intuitive signals and convince you that you are looking too deeply into it all. The intellect cannot see beyond itself, let alone how an unimaginably complex array of events synchronize together to fulfil your intention.

Active Illumination

You can gain direct access to illumination is through your passive imagination. This is through a method called 'visioning'. Recall that your passive imagination is the flow of mental energy from the Universal to the individual. That is, it comes directly from the Universal Mind itself. Your incredible imagination will do all the hard work of translating this intelligence into imagery tailored especially for you. Because of this, your passive imagination is the easiest and surest way to tune into illumination. To tap into it properly, you need to master several 'visioning' techniques.

VISIONING TECHNIQUES

The techniques all rely upon asking yourself a meaningful question and allowing your passive imagination to give you guidance. They only take a few minutes to learn, and they will serve you for the rest of your life.

1. *The Spinning Coin Technique*

The simplest of the three techniques, the spinning coin is useful for when you require a yes or no answer. It involves visualizing a spinning coin on the screen of your imagination. You then release the spinning coin to your passive imagination, which will present to you the guidance you need.

To use the technique, assign a yes/no outcome to either heads or tails of your imaginary coin. Next, visualize the coin spinning on a table appearing only as a blur. Next, hold the question in your mind, and keep gently repeating the question to yourself while the coin is still spinning. As you hold the question, release control over the image and allow it to gradually slow down, watch it start to wobble, then finally land on a face. Whichever face is showing is the response of your Higher Self to your question. Of course, you do not have to take this action. You always have the final say. Nevertheless, try following this guidance for a while and you will soon trust it to guide you effortlessly to the fulfilment of your intentions. It will always lead the growth that is required for you to enable you to align with your Higher Self.

2. *The Traffic Light Technique*

This technique is most useful for clarifying ambivalence or clearing up uncertainty about which way to act. It involves visualizing a set of traffic lights in your mind. It must have three lights: red, amber and green.

Visualize the traffic lights with all three bulbs all blackened. Next, ask yourself the question. You will see one of the lights flash a colour, which is the answer to your question.

- ✧ Red means no, stop, re-assess your options
- ✧ Amber means wait, get more information or standby
- ✧ Green means yes, forge ahead
- ✧ Alternative flashes of red and green indicates that you need to get further clarity about your question or intention.

Always trust your first impression and do not involve your intellect in the process. Receive the guidance through a peaceful detachment to the outcome. Do not use this process if you are strongly attached to a particular outcome. Your active imagination will overpower your passive imagination, and you will get whatever indication your Ego, intellect and lower self want you to see.

3. Symbol Streams

The final technique is easily the most powerful technique to channel illumination, but it requires some practice to master. You should do it as soon as you wake or as the last thing before retiring at night. You will also require a pen and paper.

1. Clear the screen of your imagination until it is perfectly black throughout your entire visual awareness.
2. Ask yourself a question that aligns with your intent decree. For example, 'What is my purpose?' or 'How can I create $100,000?'
3. Softly repeat the question in your mind. Visualize a small blurry white dot in the centre of your imagination growing larger and clearer until it morphs into an image. Intend for only one symbol to come at a time, and write/draw it as it visualizes.

The imagery that flashes in your mind will be symbolic, not literal. Recall that the Universal Mind expresses its intelligence symbolically, so you should never seek a literal interpretation of the imagery. So how do you interpret this imagery?

The key to interpreting the imagery might surprise you, but do not rule it out until you have tried it. You are going to need to relinquish your preconceptions for a moment and trust me on this one! So here it is:

You Make It Up!

That is right! The spontaneous first thoughts that flow into your mind when you think about the symbols hold the correct interpretations. This is because all of the things that you associate with that symbol will flow into your awareness, whether they are conscious or unconscious associations.

Simply ask yourself lightly and playfully what the symbol means to you. Receive the answers as spontaneous and free flowing associations. Record them. It is that simple. The moment you intellectualize the interpretation you have lost the point. Remember, this symbolism stems from the Universal, not the individual. It is holistic and contextual intelligence.

It is important that you do not ask anybody else what he or she thinks the symbols mean. They cannot decipher or interpret their meaning, as the imagery is tailor-made for you. The imagery is contextual symbolism, and can only be interpreted within the framework of your own associations.

These techniques will always give you answers that lead you upon the path of growth and transformation. Sometimes that will involve a degree of risk, but you should not be reckless. Until you have plenty of experience with the methods and trust in the experience completely, do not quit your day job or file for a divorce!

STEP 5

INSPIRED ACTION

Dreams pass into the reality of action.
From the actions stems the dream again;
and this interdependence produces the highest form of living.
- Anais Nin

Inspired Action is the final step and the ultimate goal of the entire manifesting process. Taking action shifts the energy you have generated in the metaphysical Universe into the physical Universe. In this book, though, we are not talking about any ordinary action. We are talking about Inspired Action. Inspired Action can save you years of labour or trial and error. Action taken upon the guiding light of illumination is the esoteric alchemists' true gold. When you receive illumination, and take actions aligned with this guidance, you are taking Inspired Action.

Inspired action is about expressing your intention with the minimum amount of money, time and energy. The Universal Mind can generate an infinite supply of inspired ideas and creative insights that will lead you to the effortless fulfilment of your intention. Your final task is to be prepared to act upon the given illumination.

The Universe operates upon the principles of speed and efficiency. Everything in nature follows the path of least resistance, so too does the manifestation process. When you take action that is inspired by the orchestrating intelligence of the Universe, you tap into this path of least resistance.

Taking action shows commitment. You literally prove to yourself that you mean what you say. We have all heard the expression 'actions speak louder than words'. It is an immutable truth. It is no different with manifesting your intentions. You can follow all of the steps in this process, from intention to impression to illumination, but unless there is action, there is no expression.

This diagram shows the interplay of the active and passive principle throughout the manifestation process:

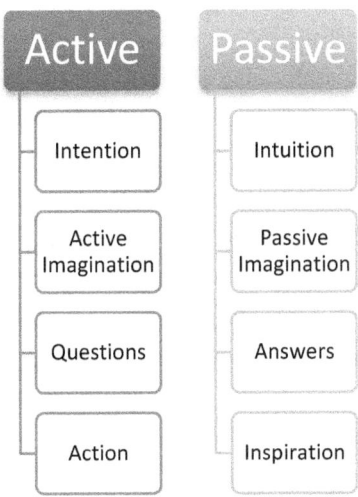

Note that action is the counterpart to inspiration. The Universe will supply you the means to your fulfilment through inspiration, but only you can take the action. Action is required to complete the circuit, to transmute the metaphysical into the physical. So where do you start?

Action 101

You start by taking the most obvious action. After you have received your illumination, you do all of the plain and obvious things you can think of and act upon them immediately. There is a lot of fresh and vibrant energy after the illumination and you need to channel this energy to vitalize your intention.

For instance, the illumination received in response to your intention to create $100,000 might be to write a book about a particular subject that fascinates you. You might begin by enrolling in a writing course, start to research your topic intensively and equip and prepare a writing workstation. You could even work out an action plan that details how much time you will spend on it and when. The intellect is the thrust behind obvious action. It will come up with the practical plans, blueprints, budgets and obvious first steps required to bring about momentum.

Taking obvious action sends a very powerful signal to the Universe. Getting this momentum going activates expectancy and reinforces the intention. Expectancy is an inherent part of intention, and taking this early action indicates that you are really expecting to see your intention through to fulfilment.

As you take action, more questions will arise which the Universe will answer with more illumination and inspiration. However, to get the process flowing, you have to begin by taking obvious action. Once you prove commitment to your intention by taking obvious action, and have done everything you can think of to realize it, you again surrender your intention to the Universe. You can still focus on the intention, but do not feel compelled to take any action towards it. This state of surrender, of releasing it back into the hands of the Universe, is critical. At the appropriate moment, you will receive the illumination you need to take you to the next level. When the moment comes, you will know what to do. The illumination will feel expansive; it will invigorate you and allow you to surmount resistance and barriers that appear to block your path. The light will literally shine upon the way!

Each step along the way, you will switch between obvious action and inspired action, between individual mind and Universal Mind. This complementary interplay of obvious and inspired action is what will lead to the effortless manifestation of your intent.

The Path of Inspired Action

Taking inspired action puts you in the resistance-free flow of joy and ease. The illumination that precedes inspired action will always be growth and joy-oriented. It never compels you toward actions that you would dread doing. Rather, it will gently prod you toward taking small steps to help you overcome your fear and self-imposed limitations.

If you continue to alternate between obvious action, surrender and inspired action, you will progress toward the realization of your intention. If you miss an inspired window of opportunity, do not be concerned. The unbounded orchestrating intelligence can easily devise a hundred more in its place. The opportunities will come back, repeatedly, in different forms and guises. There is no shortage or lack, and opportunities will never cease to flow. For as long as you hold the intention, the Universe is lighting the way and opening doors. If you hold steadfast in your intention but continue to resist, the urges will just get stronger and stronger, the impulses more compelling.

Pitfalls

The two most common pitfalls you will encounter along the path of inspired action are resistance and attachment. The Ego and intellect are the cause of both. If left unchecked, they will block and stymie the manifesting process with their practical and fragmented perspectives.

Resistance occurs when your intellect presents you with a list of reasons why it is impossible to realize your intention. It will come up with resource constraints and give you the impression you are all alone in the manifesting process. Your major task is to defy it, and continue taking action in spite of it. For instance, if you think that you will never find the time to write the book, you are encountering resistance. You must trust that you will receive the inspiration that will lead to ways that will free up the required time.

Over-attachment to the outcome is easily the biggest blockage to the manifesting process. If you are highly attached to the outcome, you are in the grips of desperation and neediness. In these circumstances, there is a tendency for the intellect to overwhelm your trust in the process and interfere.

If you are getting impatient or frustrated by a lack of progress, choose simply to surrender it again. The key is to resist trying to force things to happen. The Universe will not be micro-managed by your intellect. Simply trust that expression must follow impression, and surrender and detachment are the keys.

THE GUIDING LIGHT OF SYNCHRONICITY

When embarking upon the path of inspired action, you will often wonder to yourself 'Am I going the right way?' It is important to ask yourself this question because the Universe always answers in a special way to let you know you are on the right path. When you are in alignment with the means for fulfilment, you will experience a phenomenon called synchronicity.

In 1952, Carl Gustav Jung published a paper introducing synchronicity as 'temporally coincident occurrences of acausal events'. In simpler terms, they are meaningful coincidences that are extremely unlikely to happen by random chance. These events have four essential features that make them awe-inspiring and profound. These events have four essential features:

1. Coincidence
2. Meaningfulness to you
3. Causally unrelated
4. Extremely low probability of occurring by random chance

The experience of synchronistic events often evokes feelings of awe as they give you a direct glimpse into the orchestrating intelligence of the Universe. They occur when doors swing open just at the right time, or when the right people appear as if summoned. It might even appear to you that the entire Universe is conspiring for the fulfilment of your intention.

The Universe can effortlessly coordinate an entire array of events in ways your intellect cannot begin to comprehend. When you glimpse at the outer workings of this orchestration, you will see it as synchronicity.

When people first encounter a synchronistic event, it is common for them to feel both bewildered and amazed. This is only natural, especially if you do not have a framework to explain these grand 'cosmic co-incidences'. The important thing is not to intellectualize them; they defy the reasoning powers of the intellect entirely. Just view them as a signal that you are going the right way and be grateful for them.

Be wary of telling your friends about them. If they have no first-hand experience with synchronicity, they may conclude, quite reasonably, that you have lost your sanity! Rest assured that this is not the case. On the contrary, this is your first tangible evidence that you are coming into alignment with the Universe and your impression is expressing.

As your receptivity to illumination expands, and you master the action-surrender-inspired action cycle, you will experience synchronicity with increasing frequency. Celebrate these events and record their significance in your Gratitude Diary. In time, you will learn to trust and believe in synchronicity as being your faithful companion along the path of Inspired Action.

If you have made it this far, you should have a solid understanding of the elements of your Inner Power and the manifesting process. It is now time to apply what you have you have learnt to manifesting your Higher Purpose, your life's work. Doing so will lead you to the true source of enduring prosperity and fulfilment.

Part IV

Manifesting Your Higher Purpose

Awakening To Higher Purpose –
Discovering Your Higher Purpose –
Realizing Your Higher Purpose

Chapter Ten

Awakening to Higher Purpose

*I don't know what your destiny will be, but one thing I know:
the only ones among you who will be really happy
are those who will have sought and found how to serve.*

– Albert Schweitzer

Awakening to Higher Purpose is about connecting with your Higher Self. It is about integrating your partness with your wholeness. It is about expanding and adding value to the entire Universe by enriching the lives of others with your unique talents and passions. In the next chapter, we look at how to identify your Higher Purpose. Beforehand, let us look deeply into the notion of awakening to Higher Purpose.

The Universe is Inherently Purposeful

Recall from Part I that the Universe, before it is anything else, is comprised of holons, or whole/parts. Absolutely everything that is part of a system is comprised of holons. Humans and all other forms of life are part of this intricate and harmonious system called life. Every part serves a greater purpose that contributes the whole. Atoms support molecules, molecules support cells, cells support organs, and organs all serve a highly specific purpose to give support to life itself. This is a fundamental property of the entire Universe, both physical and non-physical. Purpose is inherent in the fabric of the Universe.

Take bees for example. Worker bees are directly responsible for pollinating 90% of our flowering crops. Albert Einstein foretold that if bees became extinct, humanity would have only four years to live. Without pollination, plant and animal life would not exist. Their existence is highly purposeful and without them, life would cease.

Each individual bee has a highly specific function to undertake within the colony. For instance, a drone's sole purpose is to mate with a queen; they do not work a day in their lives. After actualizing their purpose, they die, as this is their pre-determined destiny.

However, the human experience is an entirely different one because The Absolute has bestowed Free Will upon us. We do not have a pre-determined destiny as a bee does. It is entirely up to us how we choose to conduct our lives and how we serve the Universe, the whole. It makes no difference to the Universe if you devote your life to self-service or service to others. You can live on welfare or you can build a global business empire. The Absolute observes in perfect detachment as you exercise its greatest gift to you, the privilege of Free Will. So why do some people realize their Higher Purpose while others do not?

The Battle of your Lower & Higher Self

It is because of an eternal battle that rages within your awareness. It is the conflict between your partness and wholeness, or your lower self and your Higher Self.

The role of Ego is to give you a sense of individuality, or self-identity. It is driven by self-service and self-preservation. Its mantra is me, myself and I. On the other hand, your Higher Self, your Spirit, wants you to grow and express the seed of Divinity within you. It is driven by purpose, service to others and self-actualization. Its mantra is give that which you seek to receive.

The conflict between these aspects of Self can give rise to great inner disharmony. Ultimately, the aspect of Self that you identify most strongly with will win the war.

Do I Have a Purpose?

The answer to The Big Question depends on which aspect of Self you ask! It is really a question of perspective; the answer differs depending on your view of the world. The view from the fragmented intellect is much different to that of the Higher Self. The following table outlines the different worldviews of the Ego and Higher Self:

Lower self (Ego)	Higher Self (Spirit)
Individual	Universal
Partness	Wholeness
Isolated	Integrated
Purposeless	Purposeful
Individual	Communal
Node	Network
Cog	Machine

From this table, you can see that only the perspective of your Higher Self can reveal your Higher Purpose. Asking your lower self about purpose is an exercise in futility. So how do you find your Higher Purpose?

AWAKENING TO HIGHER PURPOSE

The process of awakening to your Higher Purpose is a transpersonal growth journey. If you have not found any purpose in your life up until now, it is because you were either not ready for the answer or have not asked the question.

The truth is that your Higher Self has always known what your Higher Purpose is. To uncover it, you need only choose to align with your Higher Self. You see, it has been waiting with infinite patience for the time you are ready. The moment you exercise your freedom to choose to align with your Higher Self, your Higher Purpose begins to unfold in perfect order.

The problem with all of this is that few people consciously wake up in the morning and deliberately choose to align with their Higher Self. Doing this just does not enter the scope of their fragmented, isolated awareness. They see what is, and identify with their Ego and intellect, and the relationships and objects that the Ego defines itself by. So how does anybody come into alignment with his or her Higher Self?

Well, The Absolute has a secret weapon. Although it cannot interfere with your Free Will, it can orchestrate events that force the growth you require to align with your Higher Self, if your soul truly wants it. If you are at the stage in your transpersonal development where you begin to ponder your place in the Universe, and genuinely want to discover and realize it, the Universe will give you the ultimate gift.

LOSING YOURSELF TO FIND YOURSELF

*An old saying has it that religion is for
those who are afraid of going to hell;
spirituality is for those who have already been there...*

- James Hollis

In an act of Divine Love, The Absolute will strike down upon your Ego with its Divine Anvil. The Divine Anvil is the only force capable of shattering the grip of the Ego, your sense of partness. The Divine Anvil is the real cause of true and enduring psycho-spiritual transformation in your life.

The spiritual literature refers to this experience as 'The Cross'. This process is the foundation for the entire notion of death and rebirth, of resurrection. To encounter The Cross is to die before you die. It signals the death of your partness and heralds a new era of wholeness, of alignment with your

Higher Self. You finally realize that you are a spiritual being having a physical experience. You awaken to Higher Power, to your Higher Self and to Higher Purpose. So what is the experience of The Cross?

The Cross experience is akin to the supernova process that you learnt about in Part I. Like stars, we 'burn' away slowly for many years in a state of ignorant bliss. Most people endure this slow burn their entire lives without ever going supernova. However, for those who truly want it, whether consciously or unconsciously, The Absolute will support the transformative growth process.

The Absolute knows that destruction is creation; it creates entire worlds with this principle. It can see the end, and look on in detachment, knowing that in spite of appearances the act is for your greater good.

In a strong fell swoop of the Divine Anvil, it proceeds to orchestrate the destruction of everything precious to you. In this act of perfectly detached love, everything that your Ego defined itself burns in the fury of the explosion. It might be your financial fortune, the loss of a long-term career identity or your friends and loved ones. It might even be a combination of all of them. In most cases, it takes anywhere from weeks to months to unfold entirely. In others, you can lose it all in a day.

However it manifests, the outcome is the same: You lose whatever it is you value the most. Unable to cope with the devastation of the blow, the Ego is temporarily shattered. With nothing to hold on to, nothing to define itself by, in the face of total annihilation, a window of opportunity opens up. This opportunity is an invitation to connect with your Higher Self, to align with your Higher Purpose, to transform, grow, and express.

Not everyone makes it through this process intact, but those who do are literally reborn. Their destruction is their creation. These survivors universally credit the experience as the most important and transformative in their entire life journey.

Your Higher Self & Higher Purpose

As the fiery embers of the Ego's annihilation cool, you will begin to awaken to your Higher Self. That is, you begin to integrate into the wholeness beyond your partness. You will start to look beyond the incessant demands of your Ego and contemplate how you can make a meaningful contribution to the Universe. As an inevitable consequence, you will begin the journey of discovering your Higher Purpose. As you do so, your significant life experiences will start to weave into a web of meaning. As the web becomes clearer, you will start to appreciate how these events shaped and forged you. You will realize that all of your life's triumphs and tribulations served to equip you with the necessary insights, experiences and skills to realize your Higher Purpose. Such is the way of the Higher Self, which sees farther and deeper than you can imagine possible. So what is your Higher Purpose?

Higher Purpose & Service

We are here on earth to do good for others.
What the others are here for, I don't know.

- W. H. Auden

Your Higher Purpose is to serve others with your special talents and passions. How you choose to do this forms the basis of your Divine Mission, which you will learn about shortly. Through your Higher Purpose, you make a valuable and meaningful contribution to the whole, to the Universe at large. Realizing your Higher Purpose is about figuring out how to apply your special talents and passions in service to others.

Your Higher Purpose is an undertaking to bring value, joy and fulfilment to the lives of others. In the process, you will create tremendous abundance, joy and fulfilment for yourself. Your Higher Purpose captures the spirit of the expression 'If you want it, give it. If you seek it, be it'.

Exactly how you serve is entirely up to you, but it will *always* leverage your unique talents, your passions and the things you love to do. It does not matter if you save people time, make them money or help them realize inner growth or harmony.

Chapter Eleven

Discovering Your Higher Purpose

You don't find your purpose, your purpose finds you.

- Dr. Wayne W. Dyer

The key to discovering your Higher Purpose is to realize that it is not something you can find. You cannot wake up one day and decide to search for it in the world outside of yourself. Any attempts to search for it will inevitably end in frustration and confusion, as the endless sea of possibilities act quickly to overwhelm even the most earnest seeker. Rather, your Higher Purpose is something that finds you. Your role in the process is to let it in, to open your arms to it, to receive it. It involves deep introspection, contemplation, and receptivity to the guidance of your Higher Self, which expresses through intuition.

The truth is, your Higher Purpose has been trying to find you your entire life but you have been hiding from it behind the veils of your fragmented Ego and intellect. Like your nose, it has been sitting there all along, just waiting to be noticed.

In what follows, you will learn four easy techniques that will help you shift your awareness within and begin the process of uncovering your Higher Purpose.

1. Ask yourself The Big Question
2. Identify your special talents and passions
3. Contemplate your childhood
4. The experience of timeless awareness

1. Ask yourself The Big Question

The key to expanding your awareness on any topic is to ask yourself the right questions. From powerful questions comes powerful focus, which results in powerful answers. The most powerful question of all is 'What is my Higher Purpose?'

So right now, take the time to ask yourself this question. Ask it out aloud, with a deliberate intent to have it answered. Feel a conviction that you know the answer, and without intellectualizing it, allow your ideas to flow freely onto the space below.

What is my Higher Purpose?
_____
_____
_____
_____
_____

Whenever you think about it, ask yourself the question again. As you go about your day, focus on being receptive to whatever cues the Universe offers you about your Higher Purpose. The most important cue that you get from the Universe will come in the form of synchronicity. As you ask yourself this question, keep an eye out for unlikely co-incidences. When they occur, take a note of them in your Synchronicity Diary. In many of my workshops, the most spectacular synchronicity stories are in response to asking about your Higher Purpose.

It is important to note when thinking about your Higher Purpose that you resist your intellects attempts to limit your vision because of practical restraints like money or time. This stage of the process is not about considering how you can make money from your service. The way you apply your talents, how much value you create and how many people you impact will determine how much money you make. For now, you need clarity and focus of intent. The inspiration for surmounting the practical and moneymaking issues will come in the illumination stage of the manifesting process.

Answer the following questions to get further clarity about your Higher Purpose.

Who would I love to be?

_____
_____
_____
_____

What would I love to do?

_____
_____
_____
_____

What would I love to have?

_____
_____
_____
_____

2. Identify Your Special Talents and Passions

Where your talents and the needs of the world cross lies your calling.

\- Aristotle

Your special talents hold the key to identifying your Higher Purpose. They always encapsulate the means for realizing your Divine Mission. The problem with special talents is that you never think they are special. They just come *naturally* to you, so you do not understand why people make such a big fuss about them. Make no mistake though, other people have been telling you what your Higher Purpose is your entire life. When you repeatedly hear people commenting on a gift that you have, rest assured that gift is a key to your Higher Purpose.

Throughout my life, people have often commented on my ability to:

_____
_____
_____
_____

If I asked my closest friend what they thought my special talents were, they would say:

_____
_____
_____
_____

Another gateway to uncovering your Higher Purpose is through your passions. Passions absorb you, enthral you, invigorate and vitalize you. They fire you up with enthusiasm, and you can undertake them tirelessly. Passion is the energy you get from aligning with your Higher Purpose. Everybody feels a passion for something, but many have difficulty articulating it.

What activities/subjects do you find yourself devoting to tirelessly?

_____
_____
_____
_____

What vision or ideal do you feel most passionate about realizing?

_____
_____
_____
_____

3. CONTEMPLATE YOUR CHILDHOOD

When we are children, we are free to create and express ourselves without restraint. There is no concern about the daily affairs of running a household, earning a living or caring for a family. Children are free to imagine, play and be. In this state, your Higher Self flows through you without resistance. That is why regressing back to your childhood is a powerful method to crystallize your Higher Purpose.

Reflecting upon my childhood...

What did I spend most of my time doing?

_____
_____
_____
_____

What activity stands out as the one that best characterizes the joy of my childhood?

_____
_____
_____
_____

What are my fondest childhood memories about?

_____
_____
_____
_____

4. Timeless Awareness

That is happiness; to be dissolved into something completely great.

-Willa Cather

When you are so completely absorbed by a subject or activity that you lose sense of time, you are in a state of timeless awareness. Entire hours can pass by in what seem like minutes. You literally get lost in yourself, and awareness stands still. This state of mind holds an important clue to your Higher Purpose. When you find yourself entering this state doing when engaged in particular subjects or activities, you can rest assured it aligns in with your Higher Purpose.

I get so absorbed that I lose track of time whenever I:

_____
_____
_____
_____
_____

I could easily spend an entire day working without a break when I am working on:

_____
_____
_____
_____
_____

The Eulogy

Another way to get clarity about your Higher Purpose is to think from the end. How do you want people to remember you after you leave the physical plane? What would you want them to say at your eulogy? What would you wish you did that you might not have otherwise done? In the final analysis, most people do not wish for Ego driven desires like bigger houses or more money. More often, what we wish for is actually greater alignment with our Higher Self.

For instance, you might wish you spent more time with your loved ones, or experienced more joy, meaning and fulfilment. Perhaps you will wish you made a meaningful and valuable contribution to the Universe. If you have never thought about, here is your opportunity!

How do I want the world to remember me?

_____
_____
_____
_____
_____

What do I want the world to remember of my contribution?
_____
_____
_____
_____
_____
_____

What do I hope people will say about me in my eulogy?
_____
_____
_____
_____
_____
_____

What do I want written on my headstone?

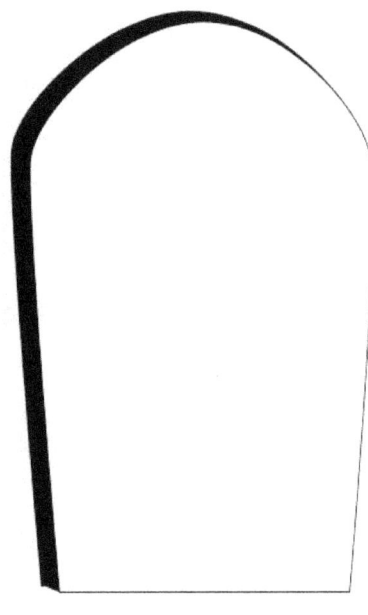

The final exercise in this chapter is to imagine what you would be doing if you were entirely free of money and time constraints.

THE LOTTERY WINNER TEST

Imagine for a moment that you hit the $10 million jackpot in tonight's lottery. All of your financial concerns have just evaporated, and you can afford to live very comfortably for at least the next decade without lifting a finger. Assuming you have travelled the world and spent some time enjoying your newfound wealth, what will you spend the next decade doing? You could choose to sit around and laze about, but chances are that will not fulfil you. The alternative is to set about infusing yourself with purpose and passion and to about realizing your Divine Mission. Assuming you choose the latter option, ask yourself the following questions:

What would I love to do if I had no money or time constraints?

_____
_____
_____
_____

What valuable contribution would I make to the world?

_____
_____
_____

Chapter Twelve

Realizing Your Higher Purpose

When you are inspired by some great purpose, some extraordinary project, all your thoughts break their bonds; your mind transcends limitations, your consciousness expands in every direction, and you find yourself in a new, great and wonderful world. Dormant forces, faculties and talents become alive, and you discover yourself to be a greater person by far than you ever dreamed yourself to be.
- Patanjali

The journey of transforming your Higher Purpose from mind into form is the single most rewarding, fulfilling and enriching action you can take. If you have done the exercises in the previous chapter, your Higher Purpose will soon begin to crystallize in your awareness. Over the coming weeks, the ideas surrounding it will become less abstract and more concrete. This process can take weeks or months; it depends on your alignment with your Higher Self and receptivity to intuitive guidance. Those who are strongly identified with Ego will often take much longer, or need to encounter the cross experience before progressing. Once you have reached a point where you feel you have refined it into a concise and tangible expression, it is time to get to work to realize it from mind into form. It is time to set about manifesting your Higher Purpose!

THE MASTER KEY TO CREATING ABUNDANCE

Have you ever heard the expression 'do what you love and the money will come?' Well, that statement is actually only half-true. It is missing the key ingredient that will actually cause the money to flow to you. That ingredient is value. To create financial prosperity in your life, you have to do what you love and *add tremendous value to the lives of others*. Through your products or services, you will impact the experiences of others in such a way that they will *want* to give you their money. Serving people through your Higher Purpose is easily the most successful way to achieve this. By leveraging your special talents and passions in service to others, you will manifest abundance effortlessly. By virtue of perfect law, the value that you create must flow back to you in one form or another.

In order to realize your Higher Purpose effectively, consider these four vital elements:

1. The intention to realize your Higher Purpose
2. Clarity about your Divine Mission
3. Manifesting skills
4. Long-term commitment

1. The intention to realize your Higher Purpose

Intending to realize your Higher Purpose is the Ultimate Intention. That is because it has within it the greatest potential for transforming your entire life experience. People living their Higher Purpose are self-actualized people. They are in alignment with their Higher Self and focus their energy on formulating ways to serve others. Money and fulfilment cannot help but flow to them in an endless flow of abundance.

This intention is the master key to creating tremendous prosperity and enduring fulfilment in your life experience. When you are doing what you love, and serve others through it, you experience the exaltation of spirit and you break free from all your bonds. As Patanjali remarked, dormant forces, faculties and talents will come alive.

Once you have gained some clarity about your Higher Purpose, the next step is to articulate it into an Intent Decree. This process may take some refinement until you are clear about your Higher Purpose. The important thing is to get to paper and allow it to develop and evolve in its own time. The following Intent Decree worksheet should assist you.

ULTIMATE INTENT DECREE

I intend to realize my Higher Purpose by...
_____
_____
_____

I intend to feel enthusiasm, passion, fulfilment and...
_____
_____
_____

I am now in the process of serving others with my ... (*unique talents and passions*)
_____
_____
_____

I love seeing myself ... (scenario of you *enacting your Higher Purpose*)
_____
_____
_____

My Ultimate Intent Decree

_____
_____
_____

2. Clarity about Your Divine Mission

When you discover your mission, you will feel its demand. It will fill you with enthusiasm and a burning desire to get to work on it.

- W. Clement Stone

Have you ever wondered why very wealthy people bother to get out of bed in the morning? They could easily spend their lives travelling the world on an endless vacation or lazing by the pool all day. Bill Gates, Warren Buffet and Oprah Winfrey are multi-millionaires thousands of times over. They do not need more money, so why do they get up every day and work so tirelessly?

The answer is simple - they are on a mission! They have an incredible sense of purpose; it emanates from every aspect of their being. Bill Gates wants us to work more productively, Warren Buffet wants to find and create value for his shareholders and Oprah Winfrey wants to inspire and inform us. They live, eat, and breathe their mission, long after their service has resulted in great personal fortune.

As W. Clement Stone points out, when you discover your mission, it will fill you with enthusiasm and a burning desire. You can think of the mission of realizing your Higher Purpose as your Divine Mission. When you align with your Higher Purpose, your Divine Mission is simply the means for expression. It is the definite plan that you will rely on to fulfil your Higher Purpose. It is what you will actually do to serve and add value to others with your special talents.

Your Divine Mission Statement

Every successful organization has a clearly defined mission statement that directs the focus of their activities. Without a mission statement, an organization can forget about its core capabilities and stray into areas that does not leverage them. They lose money and end up having to divest and refocus on what they do best.

It is the same with Higher Purpose. If you have identified that your Higher Purpose is to be a teacher, you need to be highly specific exactly what subject you are going to teach, then stick to it! This subject must be your passion; it will make your heart sing whenever you are telling others about it. Your Divine Mission is never about being a jack-of-all-trades but good at nothing. You must focus and specialize on an activity that will inspire you and motivate you through both triumph and tribulation; it must absorb every fibre of your being!

Now it is up to you to formulate a Divine Mission statement. This statement will explain how you will leverage your special talents and passions to create value for others. To formulate your statement, review your answers to all the questions in the previous chapter. With them fresh in your mind, your task is to come up with a simple statement that defines:

> *How you intend to add value to the lives of others in a way that will leverage your special talents and passions.*

It is important not to specify a particular product or service; it should be as broad as possible whilst still capturing the essence of your service. Let me share with you my personal Divine Mission Statement to help clarify things. My Divine Mission is:

Helping others find their gold by teaching them how to manifest and align with Higher Purpose.

It is my unbridled passion; I have spent thousands of hours in joyful devotion to it. Writing this book is one of the ways I have come up with to fulfil my mission. I also conduct workshops, do public speaking and run a publishing company all devoted to this endeavour. I know this is my Higher Purpose because there is nothing I love doing more than this!

MY DIVINE MISSION STATEMENT

I will act to realize my Higher Purpose by:

_____
_____
_____
_____
_____
_____
_____

Make several copies of your Divine Mission Statement and put them when you will see them regularly, such as your wallet, bathroom and work environment.

3. Manifesting Skills

Part III was devoted to teaching you a five-step manifesting method. Learning and mastering it is critical to your success in bringing your mission to life. Use the method to impress a scenario of your divine mission upon 'formless substance'. Imagine yourself living your Higher Purpose and picture the scenario in vivid detail. See yourself as an international success in whatever field of endeavour it is. Imagine your customers lining up for your services and feel the emotions of fulfilment and joy surging through you. Visualize your satisfied customers giving thanks for the way your product or service has benefited them. Be sure to dream a big dream; let your imagination run wild. After all, this is mission that you devote your entire being to realizing! Make the imagery exciting and inspirational. Follow the remaining steps of the manifesting method through, using your Divine Mission Statement to focus your actions in step 5.

Asking the Universe for Support

Ask, and it shall be given you; seek, and ye shall find; knock, and it shall be opened unto you:
For every one that asketh receiveth; and he that seeketh findeth; and to him that knocketh it shall be opened.

- Matthew 7:7-8

When you follow this process through, you will soon come to the point where you require resources, such as money and the special talents of others. At this point, remember the expression 'if you don't ask, you don't get'. It is an axiom of manifesting. Although these resources will not miraculously fall from the sky, illumination will light the path to acquiring them. The Universe has available every channel that you are open to receiving available to deliver you the resources you require.

In addition, be receptive to the support coming in forms other than money. For instance, if you require the services of a website designer that would normally cost $2,000, do not sit around waiting for the money to show up. Instead, tell everybody that you know you need a web designer, and let the Universe handle the details of fulfilment. They may agree for you to pay them a small deposit now and the balance later, or agree to a barter exchange or through an array of other possibilities.

This approach applies to the entire process; you must push through the resistance, imagine yourself surrounded by whatever you require and surrender fulfilment to the Universe. Let Universal Intelligence orchestrate a chance encounter with a financier, deliver you the insight for a creative financing option or even guide you to the perfect bank loan. The possibilities are endless, and the Universal intelligence will tailor make it to suit your specific circumstances.

If a friend or relative hears of your endeavour and offers to support you, gratefully accept their offer. If you resist or refuse the flow of support, you will stall the realization of your mission. You cannot do this alone! Open to receiving, so that you in turn can give! It is a dynamic flow of exchange, and you must not stymie the flow of support that will naturally flow to you.

If the Universe, through other people, is knocking on your door and offering support, accept it! For every minute you delay, the world is going without your valuable products or services. If you decide to start your own business and need start-up funding, offer to pay them back with interest and extra once you are firmly established. They will get as much satisfaction in seeing their resources lead to the realization of your dream as you do!

An Emissary of the Universe

By aligning with your Higher Purpose, and acting to realize your Divine Mission, you become an emissary of the Universe. Your primary employer is no longer your boss or organization. Rather, it is Higher Power. You work for yourself, the Universe and the people you serve. As a result, your expectations on who is paying for your services must change. As an employee of the Universe, you must open yourself to receiving from all of the channels it has to compensate you for your efforts. It might be heavy discounts, unexpectedly generous offers of support or just plain old serendipity. When you are receptive to the flow of abundance beyond money alone, you will open yourself to a flow of prosperity that others can only describe as miraculous.

A major benefit of working for the Universe is an unlimited line of credit that you can draw upon to realize your Divine Mission. Think of it as a loan from the Reserve Bank of the Universe. You can draw upon your line of credit for any purpose that serves the realization of your Higher Purpose. To withdraw from your account, declare to the Universe what you need and how you intend to use it. Imagine yourself as already being in possession of the money and visualize how you will spend it in realization of your mission. It will come to you at the perfect moment, and not a moment before. Bear in mind, you can only draw against it for this purpose and it must be repaid. You must repay it through your service to others! If you ask for $10,000 to set up a home office, receive it, then blow the lot at the casino, do not expect the Universe to shower you with money upon your next request!

4. LONG TERM COMMITMENT

Unshakeable commitment is critical to realizing your Divine Mission. It will take nothing less than everything you have, and then some, to realize your mission. For this reason, you commitment must penetrate deep into every fibre of your being, and compel you through resistance and toward action. This mission is a lifelong project that must absorb you for as long as you are capable of serving. Warren Buffet is 77 years old and is worth $52,000,000,000, but he still gets out of bed each day to fulfil his mission of finding value for his shareholders!

If you do not feel this profound commitment to your mission, you do not have enough clarity about it. It must strike a resonant chord with every level of your being. If you do not have this feeling, Do not take action in spite of the resistance. Instead, give yourself more time to let it come to you. go back and contemplate your answers in the previous chapter. When you hit upon it, you will *know* without doubt that this is your mission, your reason for being, and you will stop at nothing to see it realized. As W. Clement Stone tells us, you will feel its demand upon you; it will fill you with a burning desire to get about realizing it!

It is important to understand that the stages of manifesting your Divine Mission are like the phases water goes through as its temperature changes. Let us say you start with water frozen at 40 degrees below zero, it is solid. To change its state, you must put in a lot of energy to bring it to zero. As soon as it increases above zero, you will notice dramatic results as it spontaneously liquefies. Again, you add more and more energy to the water, this time in its liquid state. This time you must continuously add energy until its temperature increases a full 100 degrees Celsius, at which point it will boil vigorously.

The point is, in spite of all the effort you put in, there are only two critical stages that you see any real change. Nevertheless, the transformation happens very rapidly at the transition point. It is the same when you cross the manifestation threshold. Everything happens very quickly; do not come up only a few degrees short!

FURTHER SUPPORT

If you would like to hear more real life examples and practical insights, consider subscribing to SupaNova, the free monthly newsletter devoted to helping your manifest your Higher Purpose. You can join by visiting the website www.alchemyofabundance.org.

The Alchemist's Toolkit

Increasing Your Receptivity to Intuitive
Guidance – Centring Your Awareness in the
Present Moment

Increasing Your Receptivity to Intuition

The key to tuning into intuitive guidance is to be in a highly receptive state. Your spontaneous intuition is always offering guidance. However, in your everyday waking state you are mostly unreceptive to them. If you plough through your day in a busy rush, focusing on solving one problem after another, you block these signals. This is simply because your intellect is on full throttle; it overwhelms the subtle intuitive signals. You literally are not on right 'wavelength' to receive intuitive guidance.

However, you can practice a very simple technique in the morning or at night that will open the floodgates of receptivity. It involves accessing a special state of mind. Before we look at this state, it helps to understand the major states of awareness.

State of Awareness

We all experience four major states of awareness, ranging from deep dreamless sleep to normal waking consciousness. Each of these states is associated with a specific 'brainwave pattern' that can be measured with special monitoring equipment. The following chart shows each of these states, and how many times per second, the electrical signals in your brain are cycling each second:

State of awareness	Pattern	Frequency
Deep, dreamless sleep	Delta	0.1 - 3.9
Dreaming sleep	Theta	4.0 - 7.9
Relaxed, light trance	Alpha	8.0 - 13.9
Everyday awareness	Beta	14 - 30

The two patterns that we are interested in here are the alpha and beta patterns. Let us have a closer look at each of them.

BETA – EVERYDAY AWARENESS

In this state, your eyes are open and you are processing the stimulus, making decisions and problem solving. From a few minutes after we wake up until a few minutes before we go to sleep, this is your predominant state. In this state, the intellect thrives, thoughts are pulsing everywhere and you are on ready to deal with anything that comes your way. When you record your brainwave pattern in this state over the duration of one second on an EEG machine, it looks like this:

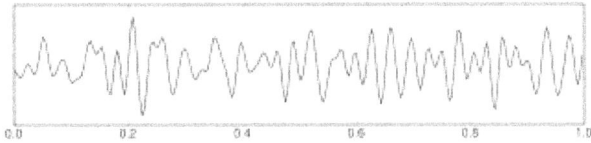

Note the sharp peaks and valleys and the relatively large number of spikes. If you count all the peaks, you will see there are roughly thirty. It is a turbulent and stormy environment of thought impulses; intuitive messages from the Universal have little chance of penetrating.

Alpha – Deeply Relaxed Awareness

When you drop the frequency of your brainwaves down by a half to a third, you enter the alpha state. You experience the alpha state first thing in the morning or last thing at night, when you walk in nature, listen to relaxing music or are engaged in timeless awareness. The contrast between the beta state is shown by the following EEG image:

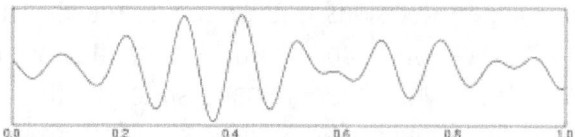

In contrast, notice how the peaks and valleys are much smoother. There are only nine peaks, or three times slower than in our everyday beta state. When you are in this, your imagination is vivid, and you abide in clear receptivity of intuitive guidance. It is a state of 'deeply relaxed alertness'. It sounds like a contradiction of terms, but you are focussed, clear and capable of intense concentration in this state. You feel a serenity of mind, but you are also receptive and mentally alert. If you have ever meditated, you will be familiar with the alpha state. If you wake up to a roaring alarm clock, you shift rapidly from Theta to Beta with only moments in

Alpha. Instead, it is better to think about how you feel after you awake from an afternoon nap or a natural rise in the morning.

The first thing you will notice is that your ability to visualize clear, detailed and vivid the images on the screen of your imagination is greatly improved. If you were to close your eyes right now, it would be take a lot of concentration to get even a vague image. That is because your mind is in Beta. The Philosophers Stone technique will take you into very deep alpha. The alpha state is the gateway to the Universal Mind!

The second thing you will notice about the alpha state is the time compression. In this state, twenty minutes may pass in what seems like only a few minutes. The deeper you go into low alpha, the more profound this perceptual phenomenon is.

Inducing the Alpha State

This following technique works best when you first wake up in the morning or just before you fall asleep at night. When you are beginning, learning how to transition from high beta into low alpha during the middle of the day is very difficult. You will be able to do this once you have mastered the technique, but for now you should stick to first thing in the morning or last thing before you retire.

Preparation

Position
There are no mystical positions or uncomfortable contortions to worry about here. Sit on a chair in the shower, lie on a bed, or rest in a recliner. It really makes no difference how you sit or lay, the key is to ensure you are superbly comfortable.

Breathing
In each technique, breathe deeply and rhythmically. This will come naturally when you are in the alpha state, but you will enter alpha more rapidly if you focus on your deep breathing.

Exit Routine
The alpha state is a subtle one, and external stimulus can easily bring you out. So that you can 'anchor' yourself more securely in the state, it helps to have an exit routine. This is simply a short phrase you say to yourself every time you leave the alpha state. I encourage you to make your own up, or you can use this one:

As I count from five to one I am leaving the alpha state. I am feeling more awake with each passing count.
5...4...3...2...1...I am now fully alert and wide awake.

The Countdown Technique

1. Close your eyes
2. Focus your eyes upward on a point between your eyebrows and about an inch outwards from your brow. This eye position is a proven and popular way to increase alpha waves, but it should not feel like a strain. If this is not comfortable for you, then look downwards instead.
3. Gently squeeze the tips of your thumb and index finger on both hands together. The reason is that each time you do it you will build a stronger association between the alpha state and this positioning of the fingers. Eventually, just pressing your fingers together like this will help induce alpha more rapidly.
4. Begin your mental countdown from 100 to 1. Allow 2 or 3 seconds to pass for each number in the countdown. The best way to do this is to 'hear' the numbers and also to visualize them on the screen of your imagination. It is easier to stay focused this way. Once you have a hang of it, I suggest you also imagine a symbol of 'The Essence' as you countdown. At this rate, you will reach 0 in 3 to 5 minutes.
5. After you have some practice, you can start at 50 or even 20 instead of 100. You will know when it's time to decrease your numbers as you gain experience with this state.
6. If you are doing it in bed in the morning that you buy a second alarm clock that is set 20 minutes ahead of your first alarm. The first few times you try it you will probably fall asleep!

When you practice this technique regularly, you will carry it forward into your everyday state. This is because you will be able to 'drop down' into alpha when you choose to. When you can do this, you enter the state of *active receptivity*. That is, you actively enter alpha in readiness to receive inspiration, imagery or intuitive guidance. The following diagram illustrates the difference between everyday awareness and active receptivity:

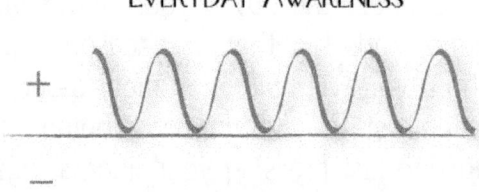

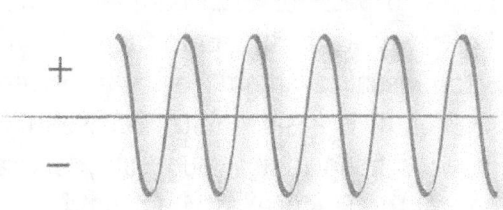

Everyday Awareness versus Active Receptivity

This state of active receptivity allows Universal intelligence to flow to you effortlessly, without resistance from your intellect. That is, you have both your active and passive polarities of mind working together. Achieving this harmony and integration between the two poles of your mind is the key to tapping into the flow of grace and effortless ease.

Centring Yourself in the Present Moment

To understand the meaning of the 'present moment', you must understand an important fact. The past and future do not exist! The truth is, your awareness unfolds in the *present moment* and it renews itself with each passing moment. Time is just an infinite series of 'nows' strung together, for all eternity. Each one of those 'nows' carries the past and determines the future.

In this framework, the *past is memory* and the *future is anticipation*. When you think about everything that you have to do tomorrow, you are anticipating. When you reflect upon what you should have done yesterday, you are recalling from memory. Either way, your awareness is not centred in the present moment. You are removed from the only moment that really exists, the 'now'.

The following diagram shows the very narrow slice of time that is the ever present now. If you are remembering or anticipating, you can be certain you are not in the 'now'.

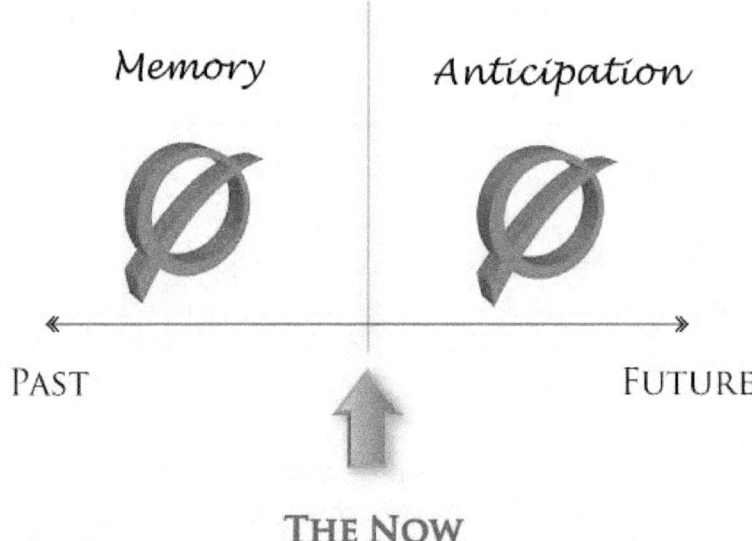

Our ability to remember and anticipate is an exquisite gift, and it is not the problem. The problem is our propensity to fixate on events that happened in the past (memory) or those we expect to happen in the future (anticipation). You may be focusing upon a terrible thing that happened to you during your childhood or the hope of great wealth and prosperity in the future. Either way, you are projecting your awareness into the past or future, with memory or anticipation. In so doing, you shift the focal point of your awareness too. You literally anchor your mind in the past or future, and you obscure the present moment!

You have full control over where you focus your awareness. When you recall memories, it is your conscious choice to direct the focal point of your awareness upon them. Your subconscious mind will faithfully restore them into your awareness with vivid clarity. It is the same with anticipating a positive outcome or a negative outcome. It is entirely up to you! Nevertheless, substituting bad memories with better ones or negative expectations with positive ones will improve your receptivity!

To open yourself to the flow of Universal Intelligence, choose to focus your attention into the present moment. Intuitive impulses are always trying to break through, but they come up against the impenetrable barriers of memory or anticipation. The greater your presence in the 'now', the more receptive you will be. Put your full focus into the 'now'!

www.ingramcontent.com/pod-product-compliance
Lightning Source LLC
Chambersburg PA
CBHW081415080526
44589CB00016B/2538